The Economic War against Cuba

Salim Lamrani is professor of Spanish and Latin American Studies at the University of Paris-Sorbonne (Paris IV) and an associate professor at the University of la Réunion. As a widely published French journalist, he specializes in Cuban-American relations. Lamrani is a member of the Center for Arts and Historical Research of Indian Ocean, University of la Réunion; the Center for Interdisciplinary Research on Contemporary Iberian Worlds (CRIMIC), University of Paris-Sorbonne; and the Interdisciplinary Research Group on the Hispanic Caribbean and Latin America (GRIAHAL), University of Cergy Pontoise. He is also a member of the French Society of Hispanists (SHF) and the scientific council of the Revista Latina de Communicación Social, of the Universidad de la Laguna, Tenerife, Canary Islands.

Besides being a regular guest lecturer in France, Lamrani has lectured widely around Europe, Latin America, and the United States, and has spoken in the company of Noam Chomsky, Ken Livingstone, Ignacio Ramonet, and Howard Zinn, among others. He is also a commentator for Radio Miami in Florida and Opera Mundi in Brazil.

Paul Estrade is professor emeritus at the University of Paris VIII and a recognized expert on contemporary Hispanic Caribbean history. He is considered the most knowledgeable French scholar of the works of José Martí, the Cuban national hero, and Ramon Emeterio Betances, the principal figure in the Puerto Rican independence movement against the Spanish Empire. Estrade is the author of many works, including *José Martí (1853–1895) ou des fondements de la démocratie en Amérique latine* (1970), which has become a standard reference work, *José Martí en su siglo y en el nuestro* (2008), and *Iniciación a Betances* (2008). He is a member of the Interdisciplinary Research Group on the Hispanic Caribbean and Latin America (GRIAHAL), University of Cergy Pontoise.

Wayne S. Smith, a professional diplomat, has been an associate professor at Johns Hopkins University since 1985 and director of the Cuba program at the Center for International Policy in Washington, D.C., since 1992. He is considered the premier U.S. specialist on relations between Cuba and the United States. Smith received a PhD from George Washington University and has served in diplomatic posts in the Soviet Union, Argentina, and Cuba, where he witnessed the victory of the Cuban Revolution firsthand. In 1961, he was appointed by President John F. Kennedy as Executive Secretary of the Working Group on Latin America, and from 1979 to 1982 he served as head of the U.S. Interests Section in Cuba. Smith is the author of many books, including *Castro's Cuba: Soviet Partner or Nonaligned* (1985), *The Closest of Enemies: Personal and Diplomatic Account of United States-Cuban Relations Since 1957* (1988), *Subject to Solution: Problems in Cuba-U.S. Relations* (1988), *Portrait of Cuba* (1991), and *The Russians Aren't Coming: New Soviet Policy in Latin America* (1992).

THE ECONOMIC WAR AGAINST CUBA

A Historical and Legal Perspective on the U.S. Blockade

by SALIM LAMRANI

Prologue by Wayne S. Smith
Foreword by Paul Estrade
Translated by Larry Oberg

MONTHLY REVIEW PRESS
New York

To Howard Zinn, in memoriam.
To Sébastien Méziane, in memoriam.
To Antonio, Fernando, Gerardo, Ramón y René,
unjustly condemned.

Copyright © 2013 by Salim Lamrani
All Rights Reserved

Library of Congress Cataloging-in-Publication Data
Lamrani, Salim.
 [Estado de Sitio. English]
 The economic war against Cuba : a historical and legal perspective on the
U.S. blockade / by Salim Lamrani ; prologue by Wayne S. Smith ; foreword by
Paul Estrade ; translated by Larry Oberg.
     pages cm
 Includes bibliographical references and index.
 ISBN 978-1-58367-340-9 (pbk. : alk. paper) — ISBN 978-1-58367-341-6
(cloth : alk. paper) 1. Economic sanctions, American—Cuba—History—20th
century. 2. United States—Foreign economic relations—Cuba. 3.
Cuba—Foreign economic relations—United States. 4. Embargo—Cuba. I.
Title.
 KF4678.L36 2013
 327.1'17—dc23
                    2013004730

Monthly Review Press
146 West 29th Street, Suite 6W
New York, New York 10001

www.monthlyreview.org

5 4 3 2 1

Contents

Every day now I run the risk of giving my life for my country and for fulfilling my obligation . . . to achieve the independence of Cuba in time to stop the United States from moving into the West Indies and, with ever greater force, into the lands of America.

—José Martí

Prologue
by Wayne S. Smith

In *The Economic War Against Cuba: A Historical and Legal Perspective on the U.S. Blockade*, Salim Lamrani presents us with an excellent summary of the American economic sanctions against Cuba, the manner in which they have been imposed for more than a half-century, and the harm they cause the Cuban people, particularly in terms of access to certain medicines. At the same time, his work demonstrates that these sanctions have failed totally to achieve their objective, which is nothing less than the overthrow of the Cuban government. Although this failure is obvious, the United States continues to pursue its objective vigorously. One might even say that this pursuit has become an obsession. As Salim Lamrani points out, Cuba does not represent a threat to the United States. The Cold War ended a long time ago and the United States has normalized its relations with China, with Vietnam, and several other former adversaries. Still, it obstinately refuses to do the same with Cuba.

The inability of the United States to interact rationally with Cuba can only weaken its position in Latin America. The global order of things has changed. There was a time when other nations (with the notable exception of Mexico) obediently followed the American example by isolating the island. But this is no longer the case. The United States is now the only country in the hemisphere that does not maintain normal diplomatic and commercial relations with Cuba. In this regard, the United States finds itself isolated, and to this day its inability to offer a more rational policy position vis-à-vis Cuba undermines its claims to global dominance.

Finally, as Salim Lamrani demonstrates, the American people no longer endorse this state of affairs. On the contrary, polls indicate that an immense majority of the American people now favor a normalization of relations with Cuba. Only a small percentage of Cuban-American hardliners, mostly in Florida, insist that the country maintain its anachronistic and counter-productive policy toward the island. It is imperative that we consider what this policy implies for the efficiency of our democratic system.

The tone of this work is serious. It provides an integral vision of what our policy toward Cuba is and has been for over fifty years.

Foreword
by Paul Estrade

This book presents a little-known reality, equivocal, even consciously obscured, and in any case, underreported by the media that are charged with selecting and analyzing information. The mainstream media, multiple but unambiguous, hide a reality that Salim Lamrani is working to restore.

Cuban "institutional specialists" and the "special envoys" in Havana certainly mention the existence of an "embargo" in their commentaries concerning the difficulties endured by the Cuban people. But they always mention it in the same way: as briefly and as vaguely as possible, through the turn of a phrase or even with a single word. They cannot deny, of course, the existence of the embargo, but in their analyses they treat it as though it hardly exists. Thus they see no need to recall its origins, its changing motivations, its illegal character, its perverse modalities, its unbearable length, and its deplorable effects. They often fail even to name the country responsible for it.

For them, the embargo is an incidental factor without importance, a mere circumstance devoid of meaning and consequence. When they deign to mention it, they turn it into an alibi or even a boon for Cuba. And, as Voltaire said, that "is exactly how history is written." But what a strange coincidence this convergence is!

Of course, one cannot contend—now less than ever—that the only cause of the present serious economic stagnation in Cuba is due to the blockade imposed by all U.S. administrations since 1960. The drastic reforms being carried out in Cuba prove the contrary. Still, some argue that the Cuban government has for decades used these unjust sanctions afflicting its people as propaganda designed to minimize its own errors and the short-comings of its system. But if this were the case one would need to explain why the United States has not ended the sanctions. Indeed, ending the sanctions is something that a near-unani-mous United Nations General Assembly asks it to do each year. In October 2010, for example, 187 states, with only two opposed (the United States and Israel) and three abstentions (Microne-sia, the Marshall Islands, and Palau) once again demanded dropping the sanctions when they voted yes on the resolution titled "Necessity of ending the economic, commercial and finan-cial embargo imposed by the United States against Cuba."

Now, either the embargo is outdated, expensive and unne-cessary, in which case those responsible should renounce it immediately, or, worse, the embargo is a convenient excuse for the Cuban government to hide its faults, in which case it would also seem judicious for its instigators to drop it.

Yet they persist in maintaining it—Democrats as well as Republicans, Obama as well as Bush—in the face of world opi-nion, against the majority opinion of their own citizens, against the vital interests of a Cuban population victimized by this state of siege. How? Why? For what reason?

Salim Lamrani is not content simply to underscore the human suffering caused by an embargo that was imposed in another century (think of the boycott of Haiti) and has ravaged the island for more than fifty years. He examines, point by point, the stages of its development and its effectiveness, places it in a historical context, and considers it from the perspective of international law. He has little difficulty in pointing out its iniquities. At the same time, he does this without pomposity and without acrimony. As is his habit, he rests his arguments on primary source materials, most of which are official documents published in the United States. In so doing, the author builds upon specific facts and dates, while presenting a wide range of official opinions. His tone is measured, even sober, but he is prolific in his exposition. Is all this too serious? The business at hand hardly lends itself to humor, but we can smile here and there while reading about the follies that the strict application of the embargo entails. In the words of American judges we learn, for example, that importing dolphins from, or selling pianos to, Cuba are actions detrimental to the interests and the internal security of the United States. Ridicule never kills. But the blockade does, certainly, by banning irreplaceable medicines from being exported to Cuba.

Call it what you will—blockade—or embargo—the economic sanctions leveled against Cuba are groundless. The pretexts Washington uses to justify them go up in smoke one by one. Furthermore, who can seriously pretend that Cuba has menaced or might represent a menace to the United States? We all know which country has been the aggressor throughout history and which has been aggressed, notably since 1959. We are also quite aware that the Bay of Pigs, where mercenaries tried to land in 1961, is in Cuba and not in California.

We also know, or should know, that when New York's Twin Towers were brought down, the Cuban government immediately offered help, and when Hurricane Katrina devastated New Orleans, Cuban authorities spontaneously offered their disinterested aid. All this occurred despite the tightening of the embargo.

The undisputed success Cuba has achieved in the fields of education and health, culture and sports, has been achieved in spite of the embargo, the cost of which, aside from the expenses generated by the various aggressions and menaces of armed intervention, was evaluated in October 2010 by the Cuban Minister of Foreign Affairs, Bruno Rodriguez, at more than $750 billion (current value) for the past fifty years. This is money that could have paid off many public debts, beginning with those of Cuba.

Despite the incongruity of this permanent state of siege and the enormity of the suffering it causes, the author does not use overly emotional language nor is he ironic nor does he resort to invective. He even shows some consideration for President Barack Obama and acknowledges the positive steps he has taken to loosen travel restrictions on Cuba. But how much more his reputation would be burnished were he to order the lifting of the embargo! The Nobel Peace Prize he received somewhat prematurely would then appear to have been justified.

France, through its representative to the United Nations, regularly votes in favor of the resolution that advocates lifting the embargo. But the commitment of France ends there. Elsewhere, in Africa or Asia, France advocates for the environment and follows an aggressive policy for "the protection of civilian populations" that it applies, unfortunately, in a quite arbitrary manner.

Salim Lamrani does not tell us what we should do. But his rigorous exposé would be in vain if friends of justice and the rule of law did not seize upon it. We must circulate this book, which is at once strong and relentless. We must indignantly pursue this state of siege, struggle against it, and contribute to its unconditional end.

Introduction

Since 1960, the United States has imposed unilateral economic sanctions upon Cuba, sanctions that affect all sectors of the society as well as all categories of its population. Since February 3, 1962, when President John F. Kennedy made the decision to isolate the island completely, these sanctions have been total. This network of sanctions is unique in terms of its length, its thoroughness, and its sophistication. It is also retroactive and applies to events that happened before the legislation was adopted, and extraterritorial: it extends to other nations and is therefore in conflict with the norms of international law. According to the U.S. government, "The embargo on Cuba is the most comprehensive set of American sanctions ever imposed upon a country."[1]

Established at the height of the Cold War in hope of overthrowing the new revolutionary government directed by Fidel Castro, the sanctions are still in effect more than a half-century later, regularly reinforced by successive administrations, Democratic as well as Republican, with the notable exception of the government of Jimmy Carter between 1977 and 1981 and, to a lesser degree, that of Barack Obama. They are based on several legislative actions: the Trading with the Enemy Act of 1917, the Foreign Assistance Act of 1961, the Cuban Assets Control Regulations of 1963, the Torricelli Act of 1992, the Helms-Burton Act of 1996, the Trade Sanction Reform and Export Enhancement Act of 2000, and the U.S. Commission for Assistance to a Free Cuba of 2004 and 2006.

The economic sanctions have a considerable impact upon the daily life of Cubans, notably in the field of health. Indeed, the United States, whose multinationals hold a virtual monopoly in this sector, also prohibits the export to Cuba of drugs produced in the United States, in violation of numerous international conventions.

The Justice Department relentlessly pursues offenders who fail to respect the restrictive regulations imposed by the Office of Foreign Assets Control (OFAC), an agency established by the U.S. Department of the Treasury, allocating for this purpose considerable resources for prosecuting individuals and legal entities that maintain economic, commercial, or financial relations with Cuba. This is to the detriment of national security and the protection of U.S. citizens from terrorist attacks, as revealed by a government report that deplores the obsessive focus on a nation that poses no threat to the United States.[2]

In fact, a significant majority of the U.S. population would like to see the economic sanctions lifted and relations with Cuba normalized. But their wishes come up against the intransigence of a minority of Cuban-born U.S. legislators, as well as the heirs to the old regime of Fulgencio Batista, who have so far skillfully managed to block all legislative initiatives aimed at relaxing the state of siege imposed on the Cuban population.

Havana accuses the U.S. government of attempting to starve the Cuban people by imposing extremely difficult living conditions, hoping these will trigger an internal revolt that will lead to regime change. For its part, Washington has never hidden its determination to subvert, by whatever means necessary, the established order in Cuba, even since the fall of the Soviet Union.

This study does not purport to be exhaustive. Rather, our intention is to sketch a brief historical overview of the economic siege enacted by Washington and bring some legal perspective to it. It aims also to shed light on the far-reaching U.S. policy affecting the development and welfare of the Cuban population. It also attempts to shed light on the reasons why sanctions have been maintained nearly a quarter-century after the fall of the Soviet Union and the end of the Cold War, a period during which Washington normalized its relations with China and Vietnam, and is on the verge of reaching an agreement with North Korea.

1.

Fidel Castro and the Triumph of the Cuban Revolution

The triumph of the Cuban Revolution in 1959 and the rise to power of Fidel Castro immediately provoked the hostility of the United States, whose faithful ally, the dictator Fulgencio Batista, was overthrown by a popular uprising. The Eisenhower administration had struggled to maintain Batista, the perpetrator of the March 10, 1952 coup, as head of state and thereby prevent a takeover by the rebels of the 26th of July Movement. On December 23, 1958, a few days after General Batista fled the island, the National Security Council, taking note of the insurgents' inevitable advance from the Sierra Maestra toward Havana, had suggested, through the voice of President Dwight D. Eisenhower, that "a military action might be needed in Cuba." Allen Dulles, the director of the CIA at the time, specified that "we must stop Castro's victory." Thus, as Christian Herter, Undersecretary of State noted, "The rejection of a regime dominated by Castro appeared to be unanimous."[3] But it was too late. On January 1, 1959, Batista fled aboard a plane destined for dictator Rafael Trujillo's Dominican Republic.

Yet, at the time, it was impossible to build anything resembling a strong link between Fidel Castro and the communists of the Popular Socialist Party. The first provisional government was composed of rather conservative members of civil society. The judge Manuel Urrutia was named to the presidency of the Republic and José Miro Cardona was selected to fulfill the function of prime minister. No communist made the list of new directors, and Washington was satisfied with the composition of the new government.[4] On the sixth of January, 1959, during a meeting of the National Security Council, the CIA underscored the fact that Urrutia was "fiercely anti-communist" and that "Fidel Castro had chosen him personally." They saw the presidential cabinet as composed therefore of "moderate and reasonable elements." The agency had also rejected the accusation of anti-Americanism on the part of the leader of the Revolution: "Fidel Castro has often expressed his desire to have friendly relations with the United States." The sharp criticisms directed at Washington were the result of "U. S. assistance long extended to the Batista regime."[5]

By February 1959, the dignitaries of the Batista dictatorship had emptied the coffers of the Central Bank and fled the island with $424 million. Washington, refusing to extradite the war criminals of the old regime, rejected a request for a loan from Cuba to stabilize its currency. This was the first sign of the hostility to come.[6]

The first economic and social measures undertaken by the revolutionary government did not sit well with Washington. The stranglehold that U.S. multinationals held over the Cuban economy was so strong that it became impossible to undertake any reforms without affecting their interests. As Ernesto Che Guevara recalled, except for land reform, all of the economic and social measures undertaken by the revolutionary government were nothing less than responses to United States aggression.[7]

The May 17, 1959, agrarian reform, one of the most advanced of the period, was predicated on the legal foundations of Cuba's 1940 constitution. It aimed to allocate to farmers cultivable land that would allow them to meet their own subsistence needs as well as put an end to the latifundia system that had long prevailed in Cuba. Indeed, Article 24 authorized, subject to compensation, expropriation for the public good. Article 90 prohibited the latifundia, thereby substantially limiting the concentration of land.[8]

As early as June 24, 1959, Washington, for the first time, began to consider the imposition of sanctions against Cuba. In an internal memo, the Eisenhower administration suggested the possibility of ending the sugar quota. The State Department openly acknowledged its objective: "The sugar industry will suffer a rapid and abrupt decline that will entail general unemployment. Many persons will be without work and go hungry."[9]

It is well to remember that in 1959 Cuba relied upon the United States for 65 percent of its exports and 73 percent of its imports.[10] The Cuban economy was, therefore, totally dependent on the U. S. market. Moreover, U. S. investments in Cuba were carried out under conditions often favorable to the multinationals. Thus, for the exploitation of nickel, the Batista regime had granted a concession to the Moa Bay Mining Company. This contract was so profitable that in just five years Moa Bay was able to obtain a return of $120 million on its initial investment. These enterprises were often exempted from paying taxes and were allowed to repatriate their profits. They therefore contributed little to the development of the Cuban economy. Between 1950 and 1960, the balance of payments was favorable to the United States to the tune of one billion dollars.[11]

On August 27, 1959, on the recommendation of Washington, the U.S. electricity firm, American Foreign Power Company, cancelled a $15 million investment. Intended to upgrade the Cuban electrical grid, the project had been in the planning stages for some time. This measure, an action that signaled increased hostility toward the Havana government, was taken following the new government's 30 percent reduction in the price of Cuban electricity.[12]

The United States was not the only country affected by the nationalizations. Most European nations—Spain, France, the United Kingdom and Switzerland, for example—also had interests in Cuba, if to a lesser degree. These nationalizations were carried out in accordance with international law that grants any nation the sovereign right to nationalize companies operating on its territory in exchange for compensation. The amount of compensation paid was based on the enterprises' most recent corporate tax returns, returns that were, for obvious reasons, often less than the real value of the assets. Agrarian reform vouchers, bearing a 4.5 percent interest rate, were issued to owners affected by nationalizations.[13]

All of the nations affected by the expropriation process negotiated with the Cuban government and accepted global compensation agreements, all with the exception of the United States. Indeed, on June 12, 1959, the Eisenhower administration demanded, as a "minimum standard," an indemnification "rapid, adequate and effective for the nationalization of U.S. assets."[14]

However, this procedure is not recognized by international law, which prohibits a third country from imposing conditions on sovereign nations, that is to say, involving itself in that nation's internal affairs. Indeed, this principle of sovereign equality has been universally accepted since the Congress of Westphalia in 1648 and is based on two essential principles, the sovereignty of states and their equality before the law. State sovereignty is expressed through the right to freely determine their internal and external affairs without infringing on other states or violating international public law. Legal equality consists of the right of any state to be considered the equal of any other in matters of sovereignty. Thus, all sovereign states are legally equal and without risk of subordination to another, independent of economic, geographic, demographic or physical factors. This principle is inscribed in Article 2 of the United Nations Charter, which states that "the Organization is founded on the principle of the sovereign equality of all members."[15]

Moreover, on December 21, 1952, during the 7th Session of the United Nations General Assembly, Special Resolution No. 626, approved by a majority vote, states that "the right of peoples to freely use and exploit their wealth and natural resources is inherent in their sovereignty and in accordance with the purposes and principles of the United Nations Charter."[16] This is what is commonly called economic self-determination, an inalienable and imprescriptible right of all peoples, which stipulates that in case of nationalization, compensation will be paid in accordance with the norms in force in the country that proceeds with the nationalization.[17]

In accordance with Article 308 of the International Court of Justice, the first source of law one should refer to in the case of conflict between nations—in the process of expropriations, for example—are international treaties.[18] Now, for the period 1959–62, no international treaty existed between Cuba and the United States that might bear on this question. We must look therefore to international custom for evidence of a general practice accepted as law. In Latin America, Mexican nationalization in 1917, Bolivian in 1952, and Guatemalan in 1953 were made based on recognized international law, and accepted as the inalienable sovereign right of states, for which "every people has permanent sovereignty over its natural resources."[19]

Moreover, according to Resolution 1803 of the United Nations, dated December 14, 1962, concerning "permanent sovereignty over natural resources," it is stipulated that "the right of permanent sovereignty of peoples and nations over their riches and their natural resources should be exercised in the interest of national development and the well-being of the state involved."[20] Thus it recognizes the sovereign right of states to nationalize foreign assets that reside on their territory.

The Charter of Economic Rights and Duties of States, approved by the General Assembly of the United Nations on December 12, 1974, also stipulates that all states have the right to

> nationalize, expropriate or transfer ownership of foreign property, in which case appropriate compensation should be paid by the State adopting such measures, taking into account its relevant laws and regulations and all circumstances that the State considers pertinent. In any case where the question of compensation gives rise to a controversy, it shall be settled under the democratic law of the nationalizing state and by its tribunals.[21]

Thus, under the international public law initiated in 1959, the process of expropriation—nondiscriminatory since it concerns all foreign assets—respected the legal agreements in force. Having been recognized as legitimate by the bulk of all nations with assets in Cuba, the compensation offered was accepted. Indeed, five agreements relating to the payment of claims were held in Cuba: with France and the Helvetic Confederation in March 1967, the United Kingdom in October 1978, Canada in November 1980, and Spain in January 1988.[22] Only the U.S. government rejected the compensation process.

2.

Economic Sanctions from Dwight D. Eisenhower to Barack Obama

The Eisenhower Government

On March 17, 1960, one month before the resumption of relations between Havana and Moscow, the Eisenhower administration made a formal decision to overthrow the Cuban government. The new U.S. foreign policy would be built upon several pillars: the cancellation of the Cuban sugar quota, an end to the deliveries of energy resources such as oil, the continuation of the arms embargo imposed in March 1958, the establishment of a campaign of terrorism and sabotage, and the organization of a paramilitary force designed to invade the island and overthrow Fidel Castro.[23]

On June 29, 1960, the oil companies Texaco, Shell, and Esso stopped deliveries to Cuba, thereby forcing the island to obtain supplies from the USSR in exchange for sugar. Responding to a new directive from Washington, the U.S. multinationals also began refusing to refine Soviet oil, thereby automatically triggering the nationalization of the refineries on the island.[24]

On July 5, 1960, Washington imposed its first coercive measures. Through Public Law 86-592, which amended the Sugar Act of 1948, Eisenhower abolished the current year's Cuban sugar import quota of 700,000 tons.[25] It should be noted that sugar accounted for 80 percent of all exports to the United States, Cuba's natural and historical market, and employed almost 25 percent of Cuba's population.[26] In response, Havana passed Act 861 on July 6, 1960, which authorized the nationalization of all U.S. properties.[27] On December 16, 1960, President Eisenhower decided that the United States would not import Cuban sugar for the first quarter of 1961. On January 3, 1961, Washington unilaterally broke off diplomatic relations with Havana and banned its nationals from traveling to Cuba.[28]

The Kennedy Administration

On March 31, 1961, the Kennedy administration extended the suspension of sugar imports until 1962. On September 4, 1961, the U. S. Congress passed the Foreign Assistance Act, which prohibited foreign aid to the government of Cuba and authorized the president to impose a total embargo on trade with the island.[29]

On February 3, 1962, by means of Executive Order 3447 and through the use of the Foreign Assistance Act and the Trading With the Enemy Act of 1917, President Kennedy imposed a total embargo on Cuba.[30] It went into effect on February 7, 1962, and, in violation of international humanitarian law, included a ban on drugs and food products.[31]

Indeed, Article 23 of the Fourth Convention for the protection of civilian persons in times of war, Geneva, 12 August 1949, and ratified by the United States, stipulates:

Each High Contracting Party shall allow the free passage of all consignments of medical and hospital stores and objects necessary for religious worship intended only for civilians or another High Contracting Party, even if the latter is its adversary. It shall likewise permit the free passage of all consignments of essential foodstuffs, clothing and tonics intended for children under fifteen, expectant mothers and maternity cases.[32]

On March 23, 1962, Kennedy expanded the embargo to all products that contain Cuban materials, including those manufactured in other countries.[33] Similarly, from August 1962, every nation providing assistance to Cuba was automatically excluded from the USAID program. On September 16, 1962, Kennedy developed a blacklist that included all ships having commercial relations with Cuba, regardless of their country of origin, and banned them from docking in a U.S. port. These measures drastically reduced the links between Cuba and the Western world and increased the island's dependence upon the USSR. This resulted in a 60 percent drop between 1962 and 1963 in trade with the so-called capitalist countries. Thus these economic sanctions took an extraterritorial turn.[34] According to the American historian Louis A. Pérez Jr.:

The U.S. embargo had a devastating effect. In early 1960, conditions had become critical in many industries due to the lack of spare parts. Almost all industries were dependent on supplies and parts now banned in Cuba. Many factories were paralyzed. Everything was devastated. Transportation was particularly strongly affected: the Ministry reported over seven thousand breakdowns a month. Almost a quarter of the country's buses were out of commission at the end of 1961. Half of the 1,400 passenger trains were inoperable in 1962. Nearly three-quarters of all Caterpillar tractors were no longer in service due to the lack of spare parts.[35]

To prevent any risk of food shortages and famine, the revolutionary government introduced a ration book in 1963.[36] Also that year, the Kennedy administration adopted a series of measures under the Cuban Assets Control Regulations designed to prevent the island from using the dollar in its international trade. It also froze all Cuban assets in the United States and strengthened the ban on travel to Cuba by U.S. citizens.[37]

The Lyndon B. Johnson Presidency

The Johnson administration extended the policy of extraterritorial sanctions against vessels making stopovers in a Cuban port. It also put strong diplomatic pressure on Franco's Spain to fall in line with most Latin American countries—with the exception of Mexico and Western Europe—and implement measures designed to isolate the island. Washington even threatened Madrid with the suspension of its estimated $100 million annual economic aid package.[38]

In February 1964, the 2,500 employees of the U.S. naval base at Guantanamo were forced to live on and spend their income on the base. These new restrictions caused a loss of an additional $5 million a year to the Cuban economy.[39]

Washington wished to make Cuba pay dearly for its nationalization process. Yet, on March 23, 1964, the Supreme Court of the United States famously recognized the validity of the Cuban nationalizations in *Banco Nacional de Cuba v. Sabbatino*,[40] which declared:

However offensive to the public policy of this country and its constituent States an expropriation of this kind may

be, we conclude that both the national interest and progress toward the goal of establishing the rule of law among
nations are best served by maintaining intact the act of state
doctrine in this realm of its application.[41]

Following government pressure, this decision was over-
turned by Congress when it approved the October 7, 1964,
Hickenlooper Amendment as part of the Foreign Assistance
Act, even though the latter, because of its extraterritorial and
retroactive nature, is in conflict with international law.[42]

Indeed, Articles 19 and 20 of the Charter of the Organization of American States stipulates:

19: No State or group of States has the right to intervene,
directly or indirectly, for any reason whatever, in the internal or external affairs of any other State. The foregoing
principle prohibits not only armed force but also any other
form of interference or attempted threat against the per-
sonality of the State or against its political, economic, and
cultural elements.

20: No State may use or encourage the use of coercive
measures of an economic or political character in order to
force the sovereign will of another State and obtain from it
advantages of any kind.[43]

Nonetheless, Washington continued its campaign to isolate
the island. Thus, in July 1964, bending to U.S. pressure, the Organization of American States imposed a total embargo against
Cuba, exempting only primary foodstuffs and medicines.[44]
These tactics were quite effective: between 1964 and 1966
trade relations between Cuba and the West plummeted from
36.9 percent to 19.6 percent of its total trade.[45] In May 1966,
the Agriculture Committee of the House of Representatives

approved a law titled "Food for Freedom Program," which prohibited the exportation of U.S. food products to countries that
maintained trade relations with Cuba.[46]

In June of 1968 the Office of Foreign Assets Control of the
Treasury Department informed Italy that all products bound
for the United States containing Cuban nickel—a significant
source of revenue for the nation—would be held at customs,
thereby forcing Rome to obtain supplies from another source
while penalizing the Cuban economy. Once again, the sanctions
against Cuba took an extraterritorial turn.[47]

The Presidencies of Richard M. Nixon and Gerald R. Ford

The coming to power of Richard M. Nixon in 1969 was marked
by the continuation of the policy of sanctions against Cuba. All
products containing Cuban nickel were permanently barred
from the U.S. market. Nevertheless, some adjustments were
made to allow the entry of Cuban cultural products, such as
those of the film industry, into the United States.[48]

Within the context of an international environment more
favorable to Cuba, which had begun to emerge from its isolation, the new president, Gerald R. Ford, who came to power
in 1974 following the resignation of Nixon (in the face of
impending impeachment), took some measures to ease the
sanctions. Indeed, in July of 1975 the Organization of American
States decided to cancel all sanctions against Cuba. After that
date, each member nation was free to maintain diplomatic and
trade ties with Havana. Thus Ford authorized a group of U.S.
businessmen to travel to Cuba through the issuance of special
licenses. He also allowed payment to Cuba of fees arising from
the landing of U.S. planes on its territory, as well as certain commercial transactions. An agreement on exclusive fishing zones
was also signed by the two nations.[49]

The Jimmy Carter Administration

The political landscape changed when Jimmy Carter became president in 1977 and decided to establish a dialogue with the island. Indeed, during his term in office Argentina opened a line of credit with Cuba and exported locomotives and railroad cars with U.S. brand names, although they were produced in Argentina. A dispute then arose with Washington because, under the terms of the economic sanctions, U.S. subsidiaries located abroad were prohibited from engaging in commercial transactions with Cuba. Thus the law that the United States intended to apply to Argentina constituted a violation of its sovereignty. After the confrontation, Carter opted for modifying certain aspects of the economic sanctions and authorized subsidiaries of U.S. companies located outside the country to enter into relations with Cuba.[50]

Carter continued his policy of rapprochement and began exploring the possibility of normalizing relations with the Cuban government. Amendments were made to the Treasury Department's Cuban Assets Control Regulations; beginning in March 1977, U.S. citizens were allowd to make trips to Cuba and the sale of food and medicines was authorized. Cubans living in the United States were authorized to send financial aid to their families on the island.[51]

In June 1977 the National Security Council chose to end the policy of blacklisting marine craft having foreign trade relations with the island. Bilateral trade transactions were authorized in the telecommunications field in August 1980.[52]

For the first time since relations had been broken off in 1961, diplomatic missions were opened in Washington and Havana.[53] In a highly symbolic move, Carter appointed Wayne S. Smith as ambassador. On January 3, 1961, Smith, then a young diplomat who had held the position of third secretary in charge of political affairs at the embassy in Havana since 1958, was the last U.S. official to leave Cuba following the rupture of bilateral relations.[54]

Negotiations also took place regarding the maritime economic zone, and several agreements were signed concerning the illegal detention of maritime vessels and aircraft. From that time on, all persons who used force (hijacking) to travel to Cuba from the United States were routinely turned over to U.S. authorities. It was not reciprocal.[55]

The Reagan Administration

The rise of Ronald Reagan to the presidency in 1981 coincided with the adoption of a more bellicose policy toward Cuba than that of his predecessor, a policy that supplanted conventional diplomacy. The new administration reversed most of the reforms that had been undertaken by Carter and implemented the Santa Fe Program, a quintessential neoconservative policy aimed at overthrowing the Cuban government.[56]

In 1981, the U.S. Senate approved a resolution prohibiting the allocation of federal resources to promote trade with Cuba. In 1982, Washington included Cuba on its list of terrorist nations and increased control over imports from countries that maintained trade relations with the island. Reagan also restricted the categories of persons authorized to travel to Cuba and imposed draconian travel restrictions. In effect, U.S. citizens were barred from traveling to the island.[57]

Disagreeing with the aggressive policy of the new presidential majority, Wayne S. Smith, then head of the U.S. Interests Section in Havana and a supporter of dialogue between the two nations, made a decision in August of 1982 to resign and leave the State Department in protest.[58]

In 1986, Reagan tightened controls on organizations promoting exchanges with Cuba and issued a blacklist of people living abroad with whom U.S. companies were forbidden from carrying out transactions. Nevertheless, faced with international protests, Reagan agreed to allow foreign companies to export products to Cuba if they contained less than 10 percent of components made in the United States. In 1988, the Omnibus Foreign Trade and Competitiveness Act, whose objective was the "reinforcement of restrictions on imports from Cuba," came into force. As a result, several dozen new maritime companies were placed on the blacklist and could no longer maintain commercial relations with the United States.[59]

George H. W. Bush and the Torricelli Act of 1992

For thirty years, U.S. diplomatic rhetoric justified the economic state of siege against Cuba by pointing a finger at the Havana-Moscow alliance. In 1992, following the disintegration of the Soviet Union, rather than normalizing relations with the Castro government, the administration of George H. W. Bush signed the Torricelli Act, which tightened the sanctions against Cuba and made it no longer possible to explain the conflict between the two nations in terms of the Cold War. Washington then brandished another argument designed to justify the intensification of sanctions: the violations of human rights in Cuba.[60]

Between 1989 and 1993, Cuban output and wages declined, even more so than during the the Great Depression. Nearly 85 percent of the nation's international trade was with the Soviet Union. Imports fell from $8.1 billion to $1.2 billion and exports decreased by 75 percent. The GDP fell by 32 percent; total consumption decreased by 27 percent and that of households by 33 percent. Capital formation fell from 25 percent to less than 5 percent of GDP, and the fiscal deficit rose from 7 percent to 320 percent of GDP. Income from the balance of payments went from $4.122 billion to $356 million. Real wages fell by 25 percent. The share of international trade fell from 70.2 percent to 25.9 percent of the GDP.[61]

The Torricelli Act, passed by Congress two years after approval of the Mack amendment that had drastically limited business transactions of U.S. subsidiaries based abroad,[62] was supposed to be the "final blow" to the Cuban Revolution.[63] Indeed, according to its author, the legislator Robert Torricelli, the Castro regime would disappear in a matter of weeks.[64]

Article 9 of the Torricelli Act forbids subsidiaries of U.S. companies established in third countries to trade with Cuba. It should be noted that 90 percent of all trade with Cuba conducted by these subsidiaries consists of food and medicines. This measure was quite effective, because after a year, all of these companies had severed their business transactions with the island. Moreover, any vessel that called at a Cuban port would be denied entry to the United States for a period of 180 days from the date of its debarkation, which was contrary to international law and once again granted an extraterritorial nature to the sanctions against Cuba. All of this constitutes an illegitimate intrusion into the internal affairs of other sovereign nations in order to regulate their trade relations with the island. The measure was nevertheless highly profitable because it cut off Cuba's relations with many global carriers that were more interested in working with the United States. The Torricelli Act also includes penalties for countries that grant assistance to Cuba. Thus, if Spain were to grant $100 million to Cuba, the United States would reduce its aid to Spain by the same amount.[65]

In addition, rhe Torricelli Act determines the economic and political model that Cuba should adopt. Article 8 provides for a multiparty system, the return to a market economy, and the privatization of many sectors of the economy. Article 1705 provides the funding for an internal opposition whose goal is to achieve regime change, something that automatically causes people who accept Washington's stipends to fall under the status of agents subsidized by a foreign power and therefore subject to long prison sentences in Cuba.[66]

In a scathing editorial of June 15, 1992, the *New York Times* criticized the adoption of the Torricelli Act, whose first victim, the editors argue, is the civilian population itself:

> Yet this misnamed act is dubious in theory, cruel in its potential practice and ignoble in its election-year expediency. . . . An influential faction of the Cuban-American community clamors for sticking it to a wounded regime. . . . There is, finally, something indecent about vociferous exiles living safely in Miami prescribing more pain for their poorer cousins.[67]

Bill Clinton and the Helms-Burton Act

On March 12, 1996, under the Clinton administration, Congress passed the Helms-Burton Act, widely considered a legal aberration because of its retroactive and extraterritorial reach. This legislation was approved following a serious incident that had occurred on February 24, 1996, off the Cuban coast when a plane belonging to the Brothers to the Rescue organization was shot down by the Cuban army after repeatedly violating Cuban airspace to drop leaflets urging the population to insurrection.[68] The organization's president, José Basulto, had been involved in the covert war against Cuba in the 1960s and had received training from the CIA. In December 2005, in a televised interview during the Oscar Haza program, *A mano limpia*, on Miami's channel 41, he admitted participating in the August 24, 1962, bazooka attack on a theater in Cuba that cost the lives of twenty people.[69]

The legislation was prepared in February 1995 and Washington waited for the most opportune moment to put it to a vote. According to Senator Jesse Helms, the United States would then be able to say "*Adiós,* Fidel."[70] The law codified all standards, regulations, and presidential orders passed since 1962, thereby elevating to the rank of law the whole arsenal of measures against Cuba that had been approved in the past. Further, it deprived the U.S. president of all prerogatives that had been permitted under the Foreign Assistance Act. Since then, only Congress can change legislation on economic sanctions.[71]

The law strengthened the economic siege by implicating other nations. Thus Title III, more specifically Section 302, allowed U.S. courts to prosecute foreign companies that took over nationalized properties that had previously belonged to persons who, at the time of nationalization, had held Cuban nationality. These persons had in fact chosen exile in the United States and had acquired U.S. citizenship after the expropriation process.[72] However, U.S. law is clear that prosecution in U.S. courts is possible only if a person aggrieved by the nationalization process was a U.S. citizen at the time of the expropriation and that the expropriation took place in violation of public international law. Neither of these two conditions were met. The Helms-Burton Act was not only flouting U.S. law but violated international law as well.[73]

Similarly, foreign investors, once having invested in Cuba, could be prevented from operating on U.S. territory. The Helms-Burton Act also prevented international financial institutions, the International Monetary Fund or the World Bank, for example, from granting credit to Cuba. This was not only in violation of the norms of these institutions but also those of the International Development Association and international financial cooperation.[74]

Because of its extraterritoriality, the Helms-Burton Act has been unanimously rejected by the international community, whose interests are directly affected. Since 1996, given the scale of international pressure as well as threats by the European

Union to bring the case before the World Trade Organization, Title III has been suspended.[75]

The Helms-Burton Act decided, among other things, future school curricula, providing that foreign instructors teach Cuban history to pupils and students. Aware of their popularity, the act prohibits the candidacy of both Fidel and Raul Castro in any future elections. It also defines the nature of a future democratic government in Cuba. This will be a "government in which the President of the United States will judge whether it meets the requirements established in Section 206." In the latter, there is no mention of human rights, freedom of expression, or of a multiparty system. Instead, it stipulates that the government must have "made significant progress in returning to United States citizens (and entities which are 50 percent or more beneficially owned by United States citizens) property taken by the Cuban government on January 1, 1959, or thereafter."[76]

As in the Torricelli Act, the Helms-Burton Act, through Article 109, allocated a budget to finance internal opposition, revealing publicly for the first time a policy that had long been hidden.[77]

On October 21, 1998, an amendment was introduced to the Omnibus Budget Reconciliation Act issued in fiscal 1999. Thus, since that date, Section 211 has prevented, for example, the French company Pernod-Ricard to market the "Havana Club" brand of rum in the United States and allows the multinational Bacardi to usurp its commercial rights. This amendment violates, among other things, the World Trade Organization's agreement on Trade-Related Aspects of Intellectual Property Rights (TRIPS) and such basic principles of the WTO as the National Treatment and the Most-Favored-Nation Treatment (MFN).[78]

Beginning in 1999, the Clinton administration decided to relax certain penalties and expand the class of persons authorized to send and receive money transfers in Cuba. Similarly, the number of U.S. and Cuban airports allowed to maintain direct links between the two nations could now include cities other than Miami and Havana. Academic, scientific, cultural, and sports exchanges were also allowed between the two countries, even those that had not previously been restricted. Washington also began to allow the sale of food and agricultural products to private entities.[79]

However, the Clinton administration applied Title III of the Helms-Burton Act to non-European nations. Thus, on June 7, 1999, the State Department sent a warning to a Jamaican company, Superclub Hotel Inc., which had plans to build a hotel complex in Cuba. Following U.S. pressure, the multinational abandoned its project.[80] Daniel Fisk, then Deputy Assistant Secretary in the Bureau of Western Hemisphere Affairs, welcomed this success: "The sanctions were not applied because the Jamaican society has terminated its business operations on the confiscated property in question. . . . The law was applied and it has worked."[81]

Similarly, on August 25, 2000, the State Department, in violation of its obligations as the host country, refused to grant a visa to Ricardo Alarcon de Quesada, president of the Cuban Parliament, who wished to attend the Conference of Presiding Officers of National Parliaments of the Inter-Parliamentary Union (IPU).[82]

The Trade Sanctions Reform and Export Enhancement Act

In October 2000, following the passage of several devastating hurricanes across Cuba and under pressure from the U.S. agricultural lobby in search of new markets for surplus production, Congress decided to adopt the Trade Sanctions Reform and Export Enhancement Act. This legislation allows for the sale of food commodities to Cuba for humanitarian reasons. Since 2002, the United States has become the main supplier of agricultural products to Cuba and thirty-eight of its fifty states have signed trade agreements with the island. Nevertheless, Washington imposes restrictive conditions on Cuba, demanding, for example, full payment in advance in a currency other than the dollar. In addition, it requires that financial transactions be conducted through a bank in a third country.[83] Thus, according to a report of the United States International Trade Commission, published in June of 2009 and titled "U.S. Agricultural Sales to Cuba: Certain Economic Effects of U.S. Restrictions," bureaucratic obstacles imposed by the Department of the Treasury have substantially limited bilateral trade. Lifting sanctions on agricultural products would lead to an increase in sales of $1.2 billion, up by 64 percent when compared to current sales.[84]

The George W. Bush Administration

On January 10, 2001, Madeleine Albright, Secretary of State under the Clinton administration, expressed her wish that the newly elected George W. Bush might be the president destined to end the Cuban regime. She thereby illustrated clearly the overall community of interests that existed between Republicans and Democrats vis-à-vis Cuba. The new tenant in the White House spared no effort to accomplish this task. Indeed, Bush has been the most belligerent White House resident since Ronald Reagan where Cuba was concerned.[85]

In February of 2002 the State Department refused to grant visas to nearly sixty Cuban officials of the state enterprise Alimport who had been invited to the United States by agriculture producers interested in trading with Cuba.[86] According to a January 28, 2002, report from the Cuba Policy Foundation, which represents the interests of the American farm lobby, trade restrictions on Cuba cost the U.S. agricultural sector $1.24 billion a year.[87] In this regard, several dozen members of

Congress called for the lifting of restrictions on food exports destined for Cuba.[88]

Similarly, the Bush administration severely restricted academic, scientific, cultural, and sports exchanges. On March 8, 2003, nearly one hundred Cuban scholars who had been invited to a scientific symposium organized by the Latin American Studies Association (LASA) in the United States were denied entry for lack of visas.[89] Similarly, beginning in September 2003, the Bush administration banned Cuban scientists from publishing articles in U.S. journals.[90]

In February 2004, Washington banned Ibrahim Ferrer, the famous Cuban singer featured in the album *The Buena Vista Social Club*, then seventy-seven years old, and four other artists from traveling to the United States to receive the Grammy Awards they had won. According to a statement from the State Department, which invoked Article 212 of the Migration Act, their visit would be "detrimental to U.S. interests."[91] The Migration Act concerns terrorists, murderers, and drug traffickers.[92]

In February 2004, the Treasury Department created a panel of three administrative judges to prosecute companies and banks that maintain trade relations with Cuba. Washington did not waste time putting pressure on subsidiaries of U.S. companies based abroad in order to ensure that they meet the restrictive sanctions encoded in the new standards. In January 2009 the Chilean retail chain D&S was forced to suspend its trade relations with Cuba following its takeover by Wal-Mart. The same month, the Treasury Department reduced from 300 to 161 the number of agencies previously authorized to make transfers to Cuba.[93]

The 2004 Commission for Assistance to a Free Cuba Report

On May 6, 2004, the Bush administration published the first Report of the Commission for Assistance to a Free Cuba

(CFAC), an entity responsible for implementing a special policy toward the island. The primary objective of the plan was to return all nationalized properties valued at more than $50,000 to their former owners. The Standing Committee for Economic Reconstruction and Privatization would take charge of the Cuban economy and all services, including education and health care. Cooperatives would be dissolved and the old latifundia restored. Similarly, social security as well as retirement and pension systems would be eliminated. A public works project would be implemented for the elderly who might still be employable. Caleb McCarry was appointed Transition Coordinator for the reconstruction of Cuba.[94]

In terms of penalties, Cubans living in the United States no longer had the right to visit their families for more than fourteen days every three years. The Bush administration also redefined the concept of family. Now, uncles, nephews, cousins, and other relatives were no longer considered a part of the family. A Cuban residing in the United States, for example, would no longer be allowed to visit his or her aunt in Cuba, nor send financial assistance to a cousin. Under the new law, only grandparents, parents, siblings, spouses, and children were considered part of the family. A Cuban living in Florida wishing to send money to his mother in Havana would not be allowed to do so if she was a member of the Communist Party. The daily amount of money that could be sent plunged from $164 to $50. Luggage could no longer exceed twenty kilos, and it became illegal to allow anyone to pay for overweight baggage.[95]

Asked about the cruel nature of these measures that divide families, Daniel W. Fisk, Deputy Assistant Secretary of State, Bureau of Western Hemisphere Affairs, made the following comments: "Once every three years each individual can decide when he wishes to travel and it is for him to make the decision. So if a family member is dying he is free to choose the right time to travel." The Human Rights Watch organization denounced these measures as "arbitrary restrictions."[96]

The commission also allocated a budget of $36 million to finance internal opposition and continues the policy of support to dissidents.[97]

The *New York Times* denounced these measures in its editorial of June 27, 2004:

> It is outrageous that the people of a communist nation have just been told they can see their relatives living outside the country only once every three years. Not only that, the types of items and amounts of money they can receive from overseas will also be curtailed, along with their exposure to visitors on cultural and academic exchanges. What's most outrageous, however, is that the government ordering this crackdown is the Bush administration, not the communist regime in Havana.[98]

The British daily *Financial Times* also criticized the new sanctions:

> This new development reflects pressure from the most extremist Cuban-American right-wing lobbies and constitutes the exact opposite of what is needed to promote opening tolerance and democracy in Cuba.... It represents a distortion in the priorities for the foreign policy. Because of what a congressman rightfully describes as a strange obsession against Cuba, resources essential to the fight against terrorism will be released for a policy of sanctions. And it is doomed to fail. In a word, Mr. Bush has been badly advised to opt for a policy which combines ideology and narrowest short-term politics.[99]

The Second Report of 2006

In 2006, the Commission for Assistance to a Free Cuba released a second plan, complementary to that of 2004. For its development, the Bush administration implemented impressive means—nearly one hundred people drawn from seventeen federal departments and voluntary agencies spent several months preparing the new document. A total budget of $80 million for 2007 and 2008 was allocated for its implementation. It provides $31 million to finance opponents to the regime, $10 million for lobbying activities to be conducted within universities, $24 million to upgrade the propaganda used against the island, and $15 million to rally the world to the foreign policy of the United States. In addition, the report envisages funding of at least $20 million annually "until the dictatorship ceases to exist." Unlike previous policies, the Bush administration set a deadline of eighteen months for the overthrow of the Cuban government.[100]

The new plan aimed to implement Titles III and IV of the Helms-Burton Act in certain countries. Its primary target was the Venezuela of President Hugo Chávez. As Cuba's largest trading partner, Venezuela is mentioned fifteen times in the report.[101]

The 2006 measures also affected the medical field. Although the major part of the world's medical technology originates from the United States, the United States would now prohibit any export of medical equipment to third countries "for use in large-scale programs [designed for] foreign patients." These sanctions clearly undermine Cuban medical cooperation with third world countries, the aim of which is to reduce the capacity of the island to provide medical services.[102]

Finally, the plan contained a secret annex that would not be disclosed "for reasons of national security."[103] In this regard, Ricardo Alarcon, president of the Cuban Parliament, expressed his concern:

For the United States, national security is a concept that
is inextricably linked to the military and to covert operations. After divulging all of this—tens of millions of
dollars more for their mercenaries, new economic restrictions and illegal actions taken against international trade
and the sovereignty of Cuba and other nations, additional punishments for Cuba as well as for citizens of other
countries—and after having made public more than two
years ago their plan that describes in minute detail their
intention to re-colonize Cuba, after all of that, what
remains to be hidden as "top secret"? What are they hiding
for reasons of "national security and effective realization"?
More terrorist attacks? New assassination attempts against
Fidel? Military aggression? When it comes to Bush and his
buddies, anything is possible.[104]

Working Group for the Implementation
of Sanctions against Cuba

On October 10, 2006, the Working Group for the Implementation of Sanctions against Cuba, a new body charged with
tightening the restrictions against Cuba, was founded with the
objective of hounding travel agencies, businesses, and citizens
that break the laws already in force. Alexander Acosta, U.S.
Attorney for the Southern District of Florida, presented the
new entity, which was composed of several government agencies, such as the Office of Foreign Assets Control (OFAC), the
Treasury Department, the Department of Homeland Security,
the FBI, the Internal Revenue Service, U.S. Immigration and
Customs Enforcement, the Department of Commerce, as well
as the Coast Guard and Border Patrol.[105]

Acosta said that strengthening the sanctions against Cuba
was one of the country's political priorities. "We want to show
clearly which federal agencies are on a state of alert to ensure

that the regulations against Cuba are properly applied." In the case of proven violations, offenders would risk penalties of up to ten years in prison and a million dollars in fines.[106]

Thus any Cuban residing in the United States who visited his sick mother in Cuba without first having obtained Treasury Department permission to leave the country, or who might stay on the island for more than the fourteen days allowed every three years, or who might spend over $50 a day during his stay of fourteen days, or send financial assistance to his cousin or aunt, or his father if he is a member of the Communist Party, could receive a penalty of ten years in prison and a million dollars in fines. Similarly, any American tourist who spends a weekend in Havana could receive the same punishment.[107]

The Obama Administration

Unlike the government of George W. Bush, the Obama administration has expressed its willingness to seek a new approach with Cuba. "I think we can move the relations between the U.S. and Cuba in a new direction and open a new chapter of engagement that will continue during my tenure," said the Democratic president.[108]

During his presidential campaign, Obama denounced the policy of his predecessor with respect to Cuba: "This is both a strategic and a humanitarian issue. This decision has . . . a profoundly negative impact on the well-being of the Cuban people. I will grant Cuban-Americans unrestricted rights to make visits to their families and to send money to the island."[109]

Obama kept his word. In April 2009, he announced the lifting of restrictions that had been imposed in 2004 by the Bush administration, an action that became effective on September 3, 2009. These restrictions had affected Cubans living in the United States who had family on the island. Now

Cuban-Americans could visit the country as many times as they liked for an unlimited period (against fourteen days during the three previous years), and make uncapped remittances to their families (against the $100 a month they were allowed before).[110]

The Obama administration also expanded the range of products that can be sent to Cuba to include clothing, hygiene products, and fishing equipment (all previously prohibited). It also allows U.S. companies to provide certain telecommunications services to Cuba.[111]

Nevertheless, the Democratic administration has not returned to the status quo in force under President Clinton. For example, on September 14, 2009, President Obama decided to extend by one year the Trading with the Enemy Act of 1917, legislation that established the economic sanctions against Cuba. In so doing, he has followed the lead of all U.S. presidents since 1962. However, according to U.S. legislation, these economic emergency measures may only be applied in case of war or an imminent threat to the national security. Neither of these two parameters could reasonably be evoked in 2009 in order to perpetuate the state of siege against the Caribbean island.[112]

Since 1996 and the adoption of the Helms-Burton Act annual renewal has not been required to maintain the economic sanctions in force. Only Congress has the power to bring them to term. Thus Obama has not taken the opportunity, highly symbolic, to act differently from his predecessors.

Moreover, Washington did not hesitate to apply restrictive measures. Indeed, on September 21, 2009, the State Department once again refused to grant a visa to Ricardo Alarcon de Quesada, invited by Barbara Lee, the president of the U.S. Congressional Black Caucus. The next day, Washington banned nearly thirty American doctors from participating in the International Congress on Orthopedics taking place in Havana. In October 2009, the New York Philharmonic, which was to appear in the Cuban capital from October 30 to November 2, was forced to suspend the trip after both the departments of State and Treasury refused to grant a license for the 150 patrons who had funded the project. Yet the orchestra had appeared in North Korea in 2008 and had also performed a concert in Vietnam.[113]

From Eisenhower to Obama, the structure of the economic siege has been maintained, although some adjustments were made, notably under the presidencies of Jimmy Carter and Barack Obama. Curiously, the most severe recrudescences of these economic sanctions—except for the Bush administration—were generally the responsibility of Democratic administrations. Indeed, in 1992, the Torricelli Act was adopted reluctantly by George H. W. Bush, who was mindful of the international complications that would result, following the declarations of the presidential candidate of the time, one William Clinton, who had praised the legislation and promised to adopt it if elected. Similarly, the Helms-Burton Act—a legal aberration according to lawyers from around the world because of its retroactive and extraterritorial character—was adopted under the liberal Clinton administration.

3.

The Impact of the Economic
Sanctions on Health Care

Economic sanctions have had a dramatic impact in the field of health. Indeed, nearly 80 percent of the patents granted in the medical sector are issued to U.S. pharmaceutical multinationals and their subsidiaries, which gives them a virtual monopoly. Cuba cannot get access to these medications due to restrictions imposed by the government of the United States.[114]

Some specific cases will permit us to grasp the many difficulties faced by Havana in order to maintain a functioning health system. For example, Cuban ophthalmological services are not able to use transpupillary thermotherapy in the treatment of children suffering from cancer of the retina. Cuba is prevented from acquiring the surgical microscopes and other equipment needed for its treatment because these products are sold exclusively by the U.S. company Iris Medical Instruments. Thus, without this technology, it becomes impossible to effectively treat this tumor.[115]

Similarly, the National Institute of Oncology and Radiobiology in Havana cannot use radioactive isotope plaques for the treatment of retinal cancer, also sold exclusively by companies in the United States. This technology, used primarily with children, helps preserve the affected eye and facial aesthetics. Faced with this obstacle imposed by Washington, the only medical alternative is to remove the affected eye and sometimes both, thereby causing irreparable injury to the patient.[116]

Additionally, Cuba finds itself in the position of being unable to acquire optical coherence tomography (OCT), which allows for the study of the retina and optic nerve. Marketed by the German company Carl Zeiss, it cannot be sold to Cuba because it contains American-made component parts.[117] Each year, nearly 1,600 Cuban patients are victims of this situation, and radiotherapy services cannot clearly define the types and extent of cancerous tumors.[118]

Nor has Cuba access to the drug temozolomide (Temodar), which is a cytostatic agent used for tumors of the central nervous system. This disease affects nearly 250 people a year on the island, including on average about thirty children. Access to this treatment would increase significantly the life expectancy and the quality of life of patients.[119]

Cuban children are unable to benefit from the Amplatzer device, manufactured in the United States and used to prevent organ rejection during surgical operations and provides for the percutaneous closure of atrial septal defects, thereby avoiding open heart surgery. In addition to cases occurring earlier, in 2010 four children were added to the waiting list for this intervention: Maria Fernanda Vidal, age five; Cyntia Soto Aponte, age three; Mayuli Pérez Ulboa, age eight; and Lianet D. Alvarez, age five.[120]

In the same way, Cuban children do not have access to the drug Sevofluorane, the most advanced general anesthetic inhaler, necessary for surgical operations, because the U.S. multinational Abbot has a monopoly.[121] There are many other similar examples.[122]

On June 4, 2004, the Office of Foreign Assets Control (OFAC), an agency of the Treasury Department, sanctioned the pharmaceutical company Chiron Corporation with a fine of $168,500 for exporting vaccines for children to Cuba through one of its European subsidiaries, even though it had been licensed to do so by UNICEF.[123]

Also in 2004, the Purolite Company of Philadelphia was fined $260,000 for having sold to Cuba ion exchange resins used for water purification. The Pennsylvania federal district court recognized Stefan E. Brodie, head of the company, as "guilty of conspiring to trade with Cuba in violation of the U.S. embargo currently in place under the provisions of the Trading with the Enemy Act of 1917 (TWEA) and Cuban Assets Control Regulations (CACRs)."[124]

On another note, in March of 2011 the United States seized $4.1 million that the Global Fund to Fight AIDS, Tuberculosis and Malaria had earmarked for Cuba. This action came on the heels of another decision taken by OFAC to freeze funds that the United Nations Program for Development had allocated to Cuba for health care.[125]

The organization Amnesty International states in this regard:

According to the United Nations Population Fund (UNFPA), treatments for children and youth suffering from bone cancer and victims of cancer of the retina were not available because they were under U.S. patent. The embargo also compromised the supply of antiretroviral drugs for children suffering from HIV AIDS. Under the terms of the embargo, medicines and medical equipment manufactured under a U.S. patent cannot be sold to the Cuban government.[126]

The Inter-American Committee on Human Rights has denounced "the impact of such sanctions on the human rights of the Cuban people." According to the agency, U.S. policy toward Havana "prevents improvements in the economic conditions of

Cubans." The committee reiterated its request that the economic siege be lifted.[127]

Amnesty International notes "the negative impact of the embargo on the economic and social rights of the Cuban population, affecting in particular the most vulnerable sectors of society. . . . The restrictions imposed on trade and financing, with their extra-territorial aspects, severely limit Cuba's capacity to import medicines, medical equipment and the latest technologies, some of which are essential for treating life-threatening diseases and maintaining Cuba's public health programs."[128]

The United Nations High Commissioner for Human Rights points out that "the restrictions imposed by the embargo contribute to depriving Cuba of vital access to medicines, new technologies and medical science, food, and treatment of water and electricity."[129]

A study by the American Association for World Health (AAWH), whose honorary president is Jimmy Carter, notes that the penalties "violate the most basic agreements and international conventions that have been put in place to protect human rights, including the Charter of the United Nations (Article 5), the Charter of the Organization of American States (Article 16), and the articles of the Geneva Conventions that regulate the treatment of civilians in wartime." A "humanitarian catastrophe was averted only because the Cuban government has maintained" a health system that "is considered uniformly as the preeminent model of the Third World."[130]

The *New England Journal of Medicine*, one of the most prestigious medical journals in the world, has denounced the negative effects of the economic sanctions imposed on the Cuban people: "The Cuban and Iraqi instances make it abundantly clear that economic sanctions are, at their core, a war against public health. Our ethic demands the defense of public health. Thus, as physicians, we have a moral imperative to call for an end to sanctions."[131]

The journal also reviewed the impact of the sanctions on the health field:

> The Cuban health care system . . . is exceptional for a poor country and represents an important political accomplishment of the Castro government. Since 1959, Cuba has invested heavily in health care and now has twice as many physicians per capita as the United States and health indicators on a par with those in the most developed nations—despite the U.S. embargo that severely reduces the availability of medications and medical technology.[132]

Thus economic sanctions, by limiting access to medical resources in Cuba, are in contradiction to international humanitarian law that prohibits all kinds of restrictions on the free movement of food and medicine, even in wartime. Therefore, they seriously undermine the well-being of the Cuban population by depriving it of means and medicines vital to its survival.

4.

United States Justice Contends with the Economic Sanctions

U.S. citizens are authorized to travel to Cuba, but they are strictly forbidden to spend a penny while there, a regulation that makes it difficult to visit the island. The Treasury Department considers any trip as a violation of the economic sanctions legislation, unless the persons who have visited Cuba can prove that they made no purchases on the island. The U.S. justice officials relentlessly pursue violators of the economic sanctions legislation and, in the process, often prove themselves to be ruthless. Here are a few examples of sanctions that have been imposed against Americans who have broken the law.

In April 1996, Kip Taylor, 73, and Patrick Taylor, 58, a couple from Traverse City, Michigan, went to Cuba aboard a sailboat. Aware that U.S. law forbids any expenditure on the island (without specific authorization), they took with them the necessary provisions for a three-month stay. When they returned they were caught by a storm and the mast of their boat was badly damaged. Rescued by the Cuban Coast Guard in international waters, they were returned to Cuba. When they approached the Treasury Department to ask permission to repair their sailboat, they found themselves up against a refusal. The U.S. authorities ordered them to abandon their boat and their two dogs and return to the United States by air, something that the couple refused to do. With the help of foreign sailors, the Taylors were finally able to repair their boat and return safely without violating the regulations on travel to Cuba. Upon their return, they were interrogated by U.S. authorities to whom they revealed having provided gauze and tape to a Cuban cook who had burned his hand. The Treasury Department then accused them of having "provided medical services to a Cuba national" and ordered the couple to pay a fine that amounted to tens of thousands of dollars.[133]

In April 2004, Wally and Barbara Smith, a retired couple from Vermont, were sentenced to pay $55,000 in fines for having stayed in Cuba for a semester and for having created a website, *Bicycling Cuba*, as well as having written a book recounting their stay.[134] The couple have expressed their opposition to sanctions again Cuba: "We think it's morally wrong to essentially wreck the economy of a country that has done nothing of substance against our interests for forty years, and poses absolutely no threat to us."[135]

On June 9, 2004, Richard Connors, a Chicago lawyer, was sentenced to three years imprisonment for having "conduc-ted trade with the enemy." U.S. justice upheld the sentence on appeal in 2006 and found him "guilty of smuggling Cuban cigars into the United States . . . in violation of the TWEA [Trading with the Enemy Act]. He was sentenced to a 37-month prison term."[136]

Also in June 2004, two residents of Key West, Florida, Peter Goldsmith, 55, and Michele Geslin, 56, were arrested for "endangering the national security of the United States." The prosecution demanded a sentence of fifteen years' impri-sonment. To justify the severity of the sentence, the state's federal prosecutor, Marcos Jiménez, posited that these "national security laws, such as we use them today, are designed to protect the people of the United States." The two friends had in 2003 organized a sailing regatta from the Florida coast to Cuba.[137] In October 2004, a federal judge, outraged by the case, decided to acquit Goldsmith and Geslin of all charges that had been leveled against them.[138]

In the same month, U.S. authorities condemned three Methodists from Milwaukee, William Ferguson, Dollora Greene-Evans, and Theron Mills, who had traveled to Cuba in 1999 as part of a religious and humanitarian group, to pay a fine of $25,000 each for "undermining national security." The Methodists expressed their disapproval of this decision: "The sanctions go against religious freedom and are discriminatory." Moreover, the sanctions were applied retroactively because, under the Clinton administration, religious travel was allowed.[139]

On August 28, 2004, Dr. Graham Simpson, of South African origin and a naturalized citizen of the United States, was fined $70,000 by the Treasury Department for having purchased six dolphins in Cuba for his water parks. The dolphins were installed on the Caribbean islands of Antigua and Anguilla.[140] Simpson did not hesitate to express his surprise: "I have always considered myself to be a British citizen who had lived in Anguilla for three years, which has no law prohibiting trade with Cuba."[141]

Similarly, on February 7, 2005, U.S. authorities condemned a Michigan couple to pay a fine of $9,750 for having donated medicines to a religious congregation during a visit to Cuba in 2001. The Treasury Department refused to consider the gesture as a humanitarian act and considered it to be a violation of the Trading with the Enemy Act of 1917.[142]

In 2006, Benjamin Treuhaft, a 58-year-old piano tuner, already condemned to heavy fines for having gone to Cuba in the past, was threatened with prosecution by the Treasury Department for having donated more than two hundred pianos to Cuba since 1995. He risked ten years in prison and a million-dollar fine. The prosecution invoked the Trading with the Enemy Act of 1917. But as the British news agency Reuters noted ironically, "Benjamin Treuhaft believes pianos are not a threat to U.S. national security even if they are played in Cuba."[143]

Thus the U.S. government monitors carefully even the slightest infringement upon the economic sanctions against Cuba. At the prompting of Max Baucus, a U.S. senator from Montana, the Treasury Department reported in 2004 that since 1993 it had made ninety-three investigations regarding international terrorism. During the same period, it also performed 10,683 investigations designed "to prevent North Americans from exercising their right to travel to Cuba." Following the ninety-three terrorism investigations, the Treasury Department imposed a total of $9,425 in fines on defendants. On the other hand, it demanded a total of $8 million in fines from American tourists who had visited the island of Cuba.[144]

5.

Extraterritorial Applications of
the Economic Sanctions

The economic sanctions against Cuba by the United States are applied extraterritorially and thus affect the citizens and companies of third countries. For this reason, Cubans call the state of siege imposed by Washington a "blockade," an operation designed to cut off completely all supplies and not simply an "embargo," which is an administrative measure or legal barrier aimed at preventing the movement of goods from one country to another.[145] Since the 2005 Ibero-American summit, all Ibero-American nations have adopted the term "blockade" to describe the economic sanctions imposed by the United States and to denounce their illegal nature.[146]

Since the London Naval Conference of 1908–1909, international law stipulates that a blockade can be used only in "wartime," that is to say, between belligerents. Since then, international legal norms do not recognize the "blockade in peacetime," which had often been applied by colonial powers in the nineteenth century.[147]

Washington acknowledges and accepts this principle of international law and has even imposed it in the past. In June of

1916, in the midst of the First World War, France created a permanent international economic action committee at the Paris Economic Conference that was designed to limit German trade with other nations. This was a response to Berlin, which had declared the waters surrounding the British Isles a war zone in February 1915. When in December 1916, the Foreign Ministry created the position of Under Secretary of State of Blockade,[148] President Woodrow Wilson expressed his reservations and took the opportunity to recall the international legal standard: "The United States does not recognize the right of any foreign power to impose barriers to the exercise of the commercial rights of non-interested nations, by using the blockage when there is no state of war."[149] Officially, the United States to this day has never been at war with Cuba, including the military intervention in the island in 1898, because the enemy at that time was Spain.

Numerous United Nations resolutions condemn the use of unilateral and arbitrary economic sanctions and extraterritorial measures. Thus Resolution 2625 of October 24, 1970, reminds us of "the duty not to intervene in matters within the domestic jurisdiction of any State" as well as "the principle that States shall refrain in their international relations from the threat or use of force against the territorial integrity or political independence of any State, or in any other manner inconsistent with the purposes of the United Nations."

The resolution also stipulates:

No State may use or encourage the use of economic, political or any other type of measure to coerce another State in order to obtain the subordination of the exercise of its sovereign rights and to secure advantages of any kind. . . . Every State has an inalienable right to choose its political, economic, social and cultural systems, without interference in any form by another State.[150]

Not all of these principles are respected by the United States. For example, Washington prohibits Cuba from using the dollar as its currency for international transactions, and the Swiss bank UBS was punished with a fine of $100 million for having received remittances from Cuba in dollars.[151] The Netherlands Caribbean Bank (NCB), a subsidiary of the Dutch ING group, was placed on a blacklist by Washington because of its trade relations with Cuba. Now NCB is prohibited from engaging in business relations with any U.S. company or citizen.[152]

Similarly, on December 3, 2004, the Treasury Department imposed a $200,000 fine on the Santander Bank and Trust, a subsidiary of the Spanish conglomerate Santander Central Hispano, located in the Bahamas, for having made remittances to Cuba in dollars.[153]

On another note, in 2004, under Title IV of the Helms-Burton Act, the U.S. government refused entry to several national leaders of the Canadian enterprise Sherritt and their families because of investments the multinational had made in Cuba.[154]

More unusual, on September 2, 2004, the Spanish airline Iberia was fined $55,000 for having transported Cuban tobacco from the Canary Islands to Costa Rica, after having made a stop in Miami. Yet the tobacco in question had never left the baggage compartment of the aircraft.[155]

Since September 30, 2004, and the strict application of rules set by the Cuban Assets Control Regulations, a Japanese car manufacturer wishing to sell in the U.S. market must first demonstrate to the Treasury Department that its automobiles do not contain even a single gram of Cuban nickel. Similarly, a French pastry concern that wishes to compete in the world's premier economic market must first prove to the same entity that its products do not contain even a gram of Cuban sugar.[156]

Sometimes the application of these sanctions takes a less than rational turn. Thus, since October 2004, any American tourist who smokes a Cuban cigar or drinks a glass of Havana Club rum during a trip anywhere abroad could be fined a million dollars and sentenced to ten years in prison. Another example: a Cuban living in France cannot, theoretically, eat a hamburger at a McDonald's.[157] The Treasury Department is quite clear on this subject:

> The question is often asked whether United States citizens or permanent resident aliens of the United States may legally purchase Cuban origin goods, including tobacco and alcohol products, in a third country for personal use outside the United States. The answer is no. The Regulations prohibit persons subject to the jurisdiction of the United States from purchasing, transporting, importing, or otherwise dealing in or engaging in any transactions with respect to any merchandise outside the United States if such merchandise (1) is of Cuban origin; or (2) is or has been located in or transported from or through Cuba; or (3) is made or derived in whole or in part of any article which is the growth, produce or manufacture of Cuba. Thus, in the case of cigars, the prohibition extends to cigars manufactured in Cuba and sold in a third country and to cigars manufactured in a third country from tobacco grown in Cuba.[158]

The Bush administration never ceased to apply the sanctions extraterritorially. On February 3, 2006, a delegation of sixteen Cuban officials, meeting with a group of American business leaders, was expelled from the Sheraton Maria Isabel hotel in Mexico City in violation of Mexican law that prohibits any type of discrimination for reasons of race or origin. Following an injunction by the U. S. Treasury Department that invoked both the Trading with the Enemy Act of 1917 and the Helms-Burton Act of 1996, the management of the multinational Starwoods Hotels and Resorts Worldwide ordered the eviction of the Cuban nationals. The U.S. laws state that no

Cuban can benefit from the products or services of an American enterprise.[159]

Moreover, on March 7, 2006, the Jamaican subsidiary of the Bank of Nova Scotia (Canada) decided to close the dollar accounts of the Cuban embassy in Jamaica and informed the embassy that no further transfers of funds in dollars could be allowed under the U.S. Patriot Act. This act violates Jamaican laws that prohibit discrimination based on origin or race, as well as Canadian law, specifically the Foreign Extraterritorial Measures Act passed to counter the intrusiveness of the Helms-Burton Act.[160]

The Japanese company Nikon has been at the heart of a scandal due to the extraterritorial reach of the economic sanctions. Raysel Sosa Rojas, a thirteen-year-old Cuban boy who suffers from incurable hereditary hemophilia, was a regional winner in the 15th UNEP International Children's Painting Competition of the United Nations Environment Program Environment (SOP). At the awards ceremony held on June 5, 2006, World Environment Day, at the Palace of Nations in Algiers, the prize—a Nikon camera—could not be given to him. Indeed, following U.S. pressure, the Japanese multinational refused to hand over the digital camera awarded by the United Nations because it contained component parts made in the United States.[161]

In January 2007, following an injunction of the U.S. Treasury Department, the Scandic Edderkoppen hotel in Oslo declined to book rooms for fourteen Cubans that had arrived to participate in a travel fair in Lillestroem, forty kilometers from the capital.[162] The chain of 140 establishments, which had been acquired in March of 2006 by the U.S. multinational Hilton Hotels Corp., explained that under the Helms-Burton Act it was forbidden to trade with any Cuban national. "We are owned by the Hilton Group in the United States and apply their decisions," declared Geir Lundkvis, the executive director of the Scandic hotel chain in Norway who, in order to comply with the

U.S. legislation, did not hesitate to violate Norwegian law that prohibits discrimination of any type.[163]

In April 2007, the Austrian BAWAG Bank, having been purchased by a U.S. financial group, Cerberus, closed all accounts for the nearly one hundred clients of Cuban origin residing in the Alpine republic.[164] Shocked by this extra-territorial directive, Ursula Plassnik, Austrian Minister of Foreign Affairs, pointed out that Austria is not "the 51st state of the American union," and that the Austrian and European laws should be respected,[165] thereby obliging the financial institution to revoke its decision.[166]

Also in April 2007, Barclays Bank instructed its subsidiaries in London to close the accounts of two Cuban companies, Havana International Bank and Cubanacan, following pressure by OFAC of the U.S. Treasury Department. Several British MPs, outraged by this foreign interference, decided to take the case to the House of Commons.[167]

In July 2007, the Spanish Hola Airlines, which had a contract with the Cuban government to transport patients with eye diseases as part of "Operation Milagro," was forced to terminate its relationship with Cuba.When it asked the U.S. manufacturer Boeing to make repairs on one of its planes, Boeing required as a condition that Hola sever its relations with Cuba, pointing out that the directive had been issued by the U.S. government.[168]

In its March 4, 2008, issue, the *New York Times* reported another example of the extraterritorial application of the U.S. economic sanctions. Steve Marshall is an English travel agent who lives in Spain and sells tourists trips to, among other countries, Cuba. In October 2007, 80 percent of his business's websites stopped working. Indeed, the site of this British citizen had been placed on the OFAC blacklist. eNom, the company based in Bellevue, Washington, that had sold him the domain name, had received an order to disable his sites, thereby causing Marshall a serious financial loss and forcing him to turn to a European server. The English entrepreneur expressed his incomprehension: "How can websites belonging to a British national operating a Spanish travel agency be affected by U.S. law?" John Rankin, spokesperson for the Treasury Department, justified the action by pointing out that his agency could conceivably sell trips to U.S. citizens.[169]

The Obama administration has also continued to apply extraterritorial measures. In August of 2009, the Australia and New Zealand Bank Group, Ltd., was fined $575 million for having conducted transactions with Cuba in dollars.[170] Similarly, on December 16, 2009, Credit Suisse was fined $536 million by the Treasury Department for the same reason.[171] In March 2010, the Treasury Department imposed a fine of $2.2 million on the Swedish company, Innospec, Inc., for having sold a gasoline additive to Cuba.[172]

Many other financial institutions have also been sanctioned.[173] In June 2012 the Dutch bank ING received the largest penalty ever sent down since the inception of the state of economic siege against Cuba in 1960. The Treasury Department punished the institution with a fine of $619 million for having carried out, among other things, dollar transactions with Cuba through the U.S. financial system between 2002 and 2007. The Treasury Department also forced the Dutch bank to break its commercial relationships with Cuba, announcing that "ING has assured OFAC that it has ended the practices that led to today's agreement." Thus, a European bank found itself forbidden by Washington from doing any business with Cuba.[174]

The Cuban government denounced this new extraterritorial application of the economic sanctions which, beyond preventing all trade with the United States (except for U.S. export of raw agricultural products), constitutes the main obstacle to the development of Cuban trade relationships with the rest of the world. Its statement emphasized that "the USA has unilaterally punished the ING bank for having, via its subsidiaries in France, Belgium, Holland, and Curaçao, carried out with Cuban entities financial and commercial transactions that are forbidden by its criminal policy of blockade against Cuba."[175]

The OFAC director, Adan Szubin, took the occasion to warn foreign businesses that still have commercial relations with Cuba. He said that this fine "is a warning to anyone who would seek to profit from violating U.S. sanctions," thus reaffirming that Washington would go on applying its extraterritorial measures.[176]

Other foreign businesses were likewise punished because of their commercial relationships with Cuba. The Swedish multinational Ericsson, which specializes in telecommunications, had to pay a fine of $1.75 million for having, through its Panama subsidiary, repaired in the United States some Cuban equipment worth $320,000. It also had to fire three employees involved in the repair deal.[177]

On July 12, 2012, the Treasury Department imposed a $1.35 million fine on the American firm Great Western Malting for having sold barley to Cuba via one of its foreign subsidiaries between August 2006 and March 2009. Nevertheless, international humanitarian law forbids any sort of embargo on foodstuffs and medicines even in wartime. Yet officially Cuba and the United States have never been in any wartime conflict with each other.[178]

In France in 2012 two executives of the U.S. travel agency Carlson Wagonlit Travel (CWT), Mano Giardini and Valérie Adilly, were fired for having sold tourist packages including Cuba. The business faces a $38,000 fine for each sale of a visit to Cuba, arousing the anger of some workers who can scarcely understand the situation. "Why didn't Carlson take Cuba tours off its reservation system when we had no right to sell them?" asked one worker.[179]

In the same way, CWT is faced with no longer being able to make the travel accommodations for members of the U.S. administration, which constitutes a substantial share of its receipts. The management of CWT made a statement on the matter: "We, including our subsidiaries, are required under these conditions to enforce the U.S. rule forbidding arrangement of travel to Cuba." So a French-based American subsidiary found itself forced to enforce the U.S. law on economic sanctions against Cuba, flagrantly violating French law.[180]

The extraterritorial application of economic sanctions contravenes the fundamental principles of international law and flouts the national laws of the countries where they have been imposed. This application clearly illustrates a reality long denounced by Cuba, namely the many obstacles imposed by Washington on Havana's relations with other nations. Far from being a simple bilateral matter, the economic, commercial, and financial restrictions that the United States imposes on Cuba are also obstacles to the development of Cuba's relations with the international community.

6.

The U.S. Government Accountability Office Report

The Government Accountability Office (GAO) is an independent government agency that works for the U.S. Congress. Often called the "congressional watchdog," the GAO investigates how the federal government spends taxpayer dollars. Its objective is to provide the bicameral U.S. Congress with "timely information that is objective, fact-based, nonpartisan, non-ideological, fair, and balanced." The work of the GAO is done at the request of congressional committees that ask it to investigate various topics. The head of the GAO, the Comptroller General of the United States, is appointed to a fifteen-year term by the president from a slate of candidates proposed by Congress. On March 13, 2008, Gene L. Dodaro succeeded David M. Walker who had resigned as head of the agency.[181]

On December 19, 2007, the GAO published a 96-page report on the consequences of the tightening of the "most developed network of economic sanctions imposed by the United States," that is, on Cuba. Customs and Border Protection (CBP) had conducted "secondary" inspections of 20 percent of passengers arriving from Cuba to verify that they were not bringing in cigars, alcohol, or medication from the island. In contrast, the average number of secondary searches of travelers from other countries was only 3 percent. According to the GAO, the focus on Cuba "may strain CPB's ability to carry out its mission of keeping terrorists, criminals and other inadmissible aliens from entering the country."[182]

The report underscores that "after 2001, the Office of Foreign Assets Control opened more investigations and imposed more penalties for embargo violations, such as buying Cuban cigars, than for violations of other sanctions, such as those imposed on Iran."[183] More important, the GAO stated that many failures were detected at "key ports of entry nationwide" that increase "the possibility for terrorists . . . to enter the country. . . . These reports emphasize that effective use of secondary inspection resources is critical to CBP's accomplishing its priority antiterrorism mission."[184] The fight against terrorism has become "CBP's top priority since the terrorist attacks of 11 September 2001."[185]

Between October 2006 and March 2007, the U.S. Customs Service at Miami International Airport made 1,500 seizures of "small quantities of tobacco, alcohol and pharmaceutical products in most cases" from passengers arriving from Cuba during inspections that lasted between forty-five minutes and three hours. However, from passengers arriving from other countries in Miami, they made only 465 seizures. These included 211 kilograms of drugs and $2.4 million in cash.[186] The report notes that a significant lack of customs staff "has created vulnerabilities in its inspection process in the U.S. ports of entry."[187]

Although there are more than twenty economic sanction programs levied against third countries, the OFAC dedicated, between 2000 and 2006, 61 percent of its resources to hunting down American tourists who traveled to Cuba without authorization.[188] OFAC conducted 10,823 investigations that concerned violations of economic sanctions against Cuba and only 6,791 investigations against all other sanction pro-grams combined.[189]

"Although the Cuba embargo is one of more than 20 sanc-tions programs that OFAC administers, OFAC penalties for Cuba embargo violations represented more than 70 percent of its total penalties in 2000–2005."[190] The study concluded that "since 2000, OFAC has conducted more investigations and imposed more penalties for violations of the Cuba embargo than for all of the other 20-plus sanctions programs the agency implements."[191] The Treasury Department has imposed fines totaling $8.1 million for 8,170 violations of sanctions against Cuba, which is an average of $992 per violation. "Most of these violations were relatively minor, such as purchasing Cuban cigars on the Internet."[192]

The GAO admits the unpopularity of the siege imposed on Cuba. The "unilateral nature of the embargo" has led most governments to oppose its application "by refusing to iden-tify U.S. travelers making unauthorized visits to Cuba via third countries."[193]

Thus, at a crucial time in the fight against international ter-rorism, the U.S. government prefers to dedicate too much of its resources to prosecuting citizens who violate the restrictive regulations imposed on Cuba. In so doing, the United States endangers its national security.

7.

The Opposition of American Society to the Economic Sanctions

Unanimously regarded as a relic of the Cold War, the anachronistic, cruel, and ineffective economic sanctions against Cuba have generated a rejection on the part of all classes of American society. The exception is the hardcore Cuban exile population in Florida and New Jersey and their accomplices, such as U.S. senators Bob Menéndez (Democrat, New Jersey) and Marco Rubio (Republican, Florida), and U.S. representatives Mario Diaz Balart (Republican, Florida), Albio Sire (Republican, New Jersey), David Rivera (Republican, Florida), and Ileana Ros-Lehtinen (Republican, Florida).

Former presidents Jimmy Carter and Bill Clinton have often expressed their opposition to Washington's policy. "I have repeatedly requested, both publicly and privately, the end of our economic blockade against the Cuban people and the lifting of all financial, trade and travel restrictions," Carter said after his second trip to Cuba in March of 2011.[194] For Clinton, the sanctions policy is "absurd" and has resulted in a "total failure" because it has not achieved its goal of regime change. He advocates a new approach.[195]

In the same way, 178 members of the House of Representatives and 38 members of the Senate supported the bill
introduced by Republican senator Richard Lugar in favor of
lifting the travel restrictions on U.S. citizens—who may travel
freely to China, North Korea, and Vietnam, but not to Cuba—
as well as lifting the sanctions.[196] Indeed, Lugar urged the Obama
administration to change course, by referring to "a policy that
has not only failed . . . but which also compromises our political
interests and our security."[197]

The powerful AFL-CIO, which brings together more than
fifty U.S. trade union organizations, adopted a resolution at
its Constitutional Convention in September 2009 that urged
Congress to lift the sanctions against Cuba and to fully normalize relations with Havana.[198]

The U.S. Chamber of Commerce, representing the business world and the country's largest multinationals, has also
expressed its opposition to the status quo. It sees Cuba as a
natural market in which other nations, such as China, Venezuela, Canada, and members of the European Union, are already
invested.[199] With the support of several members of Congress,
the agency launched an initiative calling for the lifting of trade
restrictions. "Common sense tells us to change a policy that does
not work. We have tried for 50 years without results. It's time to
find something else," said Thomas J. Donohue, president of this
umbrella organization that includes nearly three million U.S.
companies. He added, "We are losing great business opportunities in a market that lies within 90 miles from our shores. Other
countries, China for instance, are profiting from this market. It
is not too late for us to begin to recuperate our losses."[200]

The U.S. press is mostly in favor of lifting the economic sanctions against Cuba. The *New York Times*, in an editorial dated
June 4, 2009, once again condemned "a cold war anachronism
kept alive by Florida politics" and called upon President Obama
to "press Congress to lift the embargo.[201] The *Los Angeles Times*

branded the Cuba embargo "useless." "For fifty years, this country has been trying to produce regime change on the island by strangling it economically. U.S. sanctions worsen poverty [and] strengthen the Castro regime. It is absurdly contradictory to allow Americans to travel to Iran . . . but not to Cuba, which poses no threat at all."[202] The *Washington Post*, despite its conservative bent, was the most virulent toward Washington's Cuba policy:

> To this day, there is one communist country toward which American policy has been unrelentingly hostile. One communist government with which we have never even attempted détente. One communist country that we invaded without even a fig leaf of an invitation from a legitimate government. One communist country where we have never tried the seductive power of capitalism and instead have maintained a total trade embargo. And now, 20 years after communism collapsed almost everyplace else, in this same country a communist government survives unreformed and unapologetic. If any conclusion can be drawn with scientific certainty about any question in the field of political science . . . it surely is that the United States' Cuba policy has not worked. . . . And nothing has changed, except that our embargo makes us look more ridiculous and powerless than ever. The small changes President Obama announced this week will help. But abandoning the embargo as a proven failure would help more.[203]

Influential think tanks and organizations such as the Council on Hemispheric Affairs and the Cato Institute voted in favor of a new approach toward Cuba.[204] Daniel Griswold, director of the Cato Institute, issued an analysis on the subject:

> The embargo has been a failure by every measure. It has not changed the course or nature of the Cuban government. It

has not liberated a single Cuban citizen. In fact, the embargo has made the Cuban people a bit more impoverished, without making them one bit more free. At the same time, it has deprived Americans of their freedom to travel and has cost U.S. farmers and other producers billions of dollars of potential exports.[205]

The Lexington Institute, a center for political studies, released a fifty-page report to that effect under the title *Options for Engagement: A Resource Guide for Reforming the U.S. Policy toward Cuba.* The institute notes the failure and advocates a radical change of policy, stating, "Ten U.S. presidents have been unable to dispense with what Ford administration official Harry Shlaudeman called an 'intrinsically trivial' policy issue." The report recalls the positions taken by legislator Barack Obama: "In January 2004, then-state senator Barack Obama categorically rejected this policy: 'I think it's time for us to end the embargo.' At the time, he reasoned that the policy has 'squeezed the innocents in Cuba and utterly failed in the effort to overthrow Castro.'"[206] The Lexington Institute recommended to the Obama administration that as a precondition for dialogue it withdraw the conditions imposed on Cuba, reminding him that the government in Havana is not sensitive to language based on constraint.

A group of twelve senior retired military officers appealed to Obama on April 13, 2009, urging him to support and sign the bill, introduced by Democratic congressman Bill Delahunt, that would allow U.S. citizens to travel to Cuba, using the arguments of Senator Lugar: "The embargo has caused a significant diplomatic movement against the policy of the United States. As military professionals, we understand that the interests of the United States are better attended to when the country is capable of attracting the support of other nations to our cause," they said. "Throughout the world, leaders are demanding a real political change based on the hopes you inspired in your campaign. They add that Cuba provides a handier element to demonstrate that change, and it would be a maneuver that would be deeply etched into the minds of our partners and rivals throughout the world," they concluded.[207]

The American public is largely in favor of normalizing relations between Washington and Havana. According to a CNN poll of April 10, 2009, 64 percent of U.S. citizens opposed economic sanctions against Cuba. The Gallup Institute conducted the same survey on April 24, 2009, and received the same percentage. According to Orbitz Worldwide, one of the largest online travel agencies, 67 percent of all U.S. residents want to vacation in Cuba and 72 percent believe that "tourism to Cuba would have a positive impact on the daily life of the Cuban people."[208]

Clearly, a consensus exists within American society that favors a lifting of the economic sanctions and the normalization of relations between Washington and Havana. The acknowledged failure of an aggressive policy imposed more than half a century ago should convince the Obama administration and the U.S. Congress to adjust their strategy in a manner that echoes the will of the American public.

8.

Attempted Genocide?

The Cuban authorities condemn economic sanctions in the strongest terms. According to Havana, it is a "genocidal policy."[209] To justify its position, Cuba bases its argument on two elements: the Geneva Convention and a U.S. memorandum dated April 6, 1960—three months before the imposition of the first economic retaliation.

The Convention on the Prevention and Punishment of the Crime of Genocide of December 9, 1948, states in Article II that "in the present Convention, genocide means any of the following acts, committed with intent to destroy, in whole or in part, a national, ethnical, racial or religious group as such." Points that follow allude to "causing serious bodily or mental harm to members of the group" and "deliberately inflicting on the group conditions of life calculated to bring about its physical destruction in whole or in part."[210]

On April 6, 1960, Lester D. Mallory, Deputy Assistant Secretary of State for Inter-American Affairs, noted in an internal memorandum to Roy R. Rubottom Jr., then the Assistant Secretary of State for Inter-American affairs, the purpose of economic sanctions:

The majority of Cubans support Castro. There is no effective political opposition. . . . The only foreseeable means of alienating internal support is through disenchantment and disaffection based on economic dissatisfaction and hardship. . . . every possible means should be undertaken promptly to weaken the economic life of Cuba . . . a line of action which . . . makes the greatest inroads in denying money and supplies to Cuba, to decrease monetary and real wages, to bring about hunger, desperation and overthrow of government.[211]

According to Cuban authorities, this is the objective of the economic sanctions and the reason for maintaining them over two decades after the end of the Cold War. The former Cuban Minister of Foreign Affairs, Felipe Pérez Roque, has denounced this state of affairs before the United Nations and provided an interpretation:

Why does the U.S. government not lift the blockade against Cuba? I will answer: because it is afraid. It fears our example. It knows that if the blockade were lifted, Cuba's economic and social development would be dizzying. It knows that we would demonstrate even more so than now, the possibilities of Cuban socialism, all the potential not yet fully deployed of a country without discrimination of any kind, with social justice and human rights for all citizens, and not just for the few. It is the government of a great and powerful empire, but it fears the example of this small insurgent island.[212]

Thus, in the light of international conventions, the United States imposes on the Cuban population living conditions that seriously undermine their well-being and their physical and mental security.

Conclusion

More than half a century after their imposition, U.S. economic sanctions have cost Cuba more than $751 billion. They affect all sectors of Cuban society and all categories of the population, especially the most vulnerable: children, the elderly, and women.[213] Over 70 percent of all Cubans have lived in a climate of permanent economic hostility.

In 2011, during the annual meeting of the United Nations General Assembly, 185 out of 192 countries condemned, for the twentieth consecutive year, the economic siege imposed on the Caribbean island.[214] The international community has called on the United States, so far without success, to end its policy of ostracism, which is the main obstacle to Cuba's national development as well as contrary to the UN Charter and international law.[215]

The diplomatic rhetoric used to justify U.S. hostility toward Cuba has changed over time. Initially, nationalization and compensation constituted the bone of contention. Subsequently, it was Cuba's alliance with the Soviet Union that became the main obstacle to normalizing relations between the two countries. Then, in the 1970s and 1980s, it was Cuban intervention in

Africa, specifically in Angola and Namibia, actions undertaken to help national liberation movements gain independence and to fight against apartheid in South Africa, that aroused the ire of Washington.[216] Finally, since the collapse of the Soviet Union, Washington has flaunted the argument of democracy and human rights in order to maintain its economic stranglehold over the Cuban nation.

In fact, to grasp Washington's real purpose in its relations with Cuba, it is necessary to go back to the nineteenth century and heed the warnings of José Martí, apostle and national hero, who warned the peoples of Latin America against a "convulsed and brutal North," a North that aspired to annex the Caribbean island and dominate the continent.[217] Long in the crosshairs of American expansionism, the island of Cuba, because of its geostrategic position and its natural resources, has always whetted the appetite of the United States. Washington's intervention in the second Cuban War of Independence of 1898 turned Cuba into a protectorate, dependent upon U.S. stewardship. This was a state of affairs that lasted until the advent of the Cuban Revolution on January 1, 1959, at which point the United States lost all control over the destiny of the Caribbean nation. From Dwight D. Eisenhower to Obama, no U.S. government has accepted the possibility of a sovereign and independent Cuba, a state of affairs that explains the imposition of economic sanctions in 1960, sanctions that have continued over the two decades that have followed the "end of history."[218]

The state of economic siege of which the Cuban people are victims reminds us that the United States—by applying wartime measures in times of peace against a nation that has never been a threat to its national security—apparently has still not abandoned its old colonial aspiration of integrating Cuba into the U.S. Washington refuses to acknowledge the reality of a Latin American nation finally emancipated from heavy-handed U.S. guardianship and, in all likelihood, does not accept that national sovereignty in Cuba is the sole and exclusive heritage of the Cuban people. The economic sanctions also demonstrate that the struggle for Cuban self-determination, begun in 1868 by Carlos Manuel de Céspedes, father of the country, is a daily battle that is far from won. Martí, both a visionary and a man of his own time, had predicted it: "Freedom costs dearly, and it is necessary either to resign yourself to live without it or decide to pay the price."[219] The preservation of Cuban independence and identity comes, it appears, with a price.

APPENDIX 1

UN General Assembly Votes on U.S. Economic Sanctions against Cuba[220]

YEAR	IN FAVOR	AGAINST	ABSTENTION	NATIONS VOTING AGAINST
1992	59	3	71	United States, Israel, Romania
1993	88	4	57	United States, Israel, Albania, Paraguay
1994	101	2	48	United States, Israel
1995	117	3	38	United States, Israel, Uzbekistan
1996	137	3	25	United States, Israel, Uzbekistan
1997	143	3	17	United States, Israel, Uzbekistan
1998	157	2	12	United States, Israel
1999	155	2	8	United States, Israel
2000	167	3	4	United States, Israel, Marshall Islands
2001	167	3	3	United States, Israel, Marshall Islands
2002	173	3	4	United States, Israel, Marshall Islands
2003	179	3	2	United States, Israel, Marshall Islands
2004	179	4	7	United States, Israel, Marshall Islands, Palau
2005	182	4	1	United States, Israel, Marshall Islands, Palau
2006	183	4	1	United States, Israel, Marshall Islands, Palau
2007	184	4	1	United States, Israel, Marshall Islands, Palau
2008	185	3	2	United States, Israel, Palau
2009	187	3	2	United States, Israel, Palau
2010	187	2	3	United States, Israel
2011	186	2	3	United States, Israel

UN General Assembly Vote in 2011: Balance [Assessment] and Declarations[221]

SPEAKERS DENOUNCE CUBAN EMBARGO AS "SAD ECHO"
OF FAILED COLD WAR POLITICS;

GENERAL ASSEMBLY, FOR TWENTIETH YEAR,
DEMANDS LIFTING OF ECONOMIC BLOCKADE

OBAMA ADMINISTRATION SPEAKING WITH VOICE
OF REPUBLICAN PREDECESSORS, CUBAN FOREIGN
MINISTER SAYS OF WASHINGTON'S "WORN-OUT,
REPETITIVE POSITION"

DRAWING PARALLELS TO recent political uprisings in defense of freedom and self-determination, General Assembly delegates today again denounced the decades-old economic, commercial and financial blockade imposed by the United States on Cuba, voting overwhelmingly to adopt the world body's twentieth consecutive resolution calling for an end to the measures. The resolution—adopted by a recorded vote of 186 in favor to two against (United States, Israel), with three abstentions (Marshall Islands, Federated States of Micronesia, Palau)—reaffirmed the sovereign equality of States, non-intervention in their internal affairs and freedom of trade and navigation as paramount to the conduct of international affairs.

By the text, the Assembly expressed concern at the continued application of the 1996 Helms-Burton Act—which extended the embargo's reach to countries trading with Cuba—and whose extraterritorial effects impacted both State sovereignty and the legitimate interests of entities or persons under their jurisdiction. It reiterated the call on States to refrain from applying such measures, in line with their obligations under the United Nations Charter, urging those that had applied such laws to repeal or invalidate them as soon as possible.

Introducing the resolution before the vote, Bruno Eduardo Rodríguez Parilla, Minister for Foreign Affairs of Cuba, said that the United States' "hostile and aggressive" policy had not changed for the last fifty years. Rather, Washington had taken measures to strengthen its "siege" on his island nation in a "cruel and opportunistic" manner. Cuba was still unable to freely export or import products with the United States, while Cuban companies were banned from trading with American companies or their subsidiaries in third-party States.

In addition, entrepreneurs interested in investing in Cuba could not do so, hampering the economic development of the nation. The total direct economic damage imposed by the blockade was estimated to exceed $975 billion, he said, and even humanitarian aid was restricted, leading to suffering among the Cuban people.

In 1991, when the General Assembly had first decided to include the current item in its agenda, it had seemed impossible that the discussion would continue twenty years later, Parilla said. Indeed, for the two decades the Assembly had been calling for an end to the embargo, the United States had not heeded to the majority opinion of Member States. He recalled that United States President Barack Obama had recently responded with a "noncommittal refusal" to an offer made by the Cuban Government to hold a dialogue on items on the bilateral agenda, preferring, it seemed, to stick to the same worn-out, repetitive position anchored in the past. Nevertheless, Cuba's proposal to move toward normalization of relations and to expand bilateral cooperation with the United States still stood.

Taking the floor immediately after that address, the United States' delegate countered that his Government was, in fact, open to a new relationship with Cuba, which could begin if the Cuban Government began to respect the human rights of its citizens. The resolution before the Assembly did not reflect current realities, he said; that text, with its "stale rhetoric" was designed to "confuse and obscure" the real relationship between the United States and Cuba.

Indeed, he said, this annual exercise by the Assembly attempted, "to no good end," to obscure some fundamental truths. The Cuban Government's own policy was the largest obstacle to the country's own development, concentrating political and economic decisions in the hands of the few and stifling economic growth.

The United States was, in fact, a leading source of food and humanitarian aid to Cuba. He said that in 2010 alone, the island nation had received some $3.5 billion in total sales of United States goods, including some $360 million in agricultural products. The United States had also authorized $861 million in humanitarian assistance to Cuba. Moreover, he emphasized, it was the Cuban Government that had denied its citizens the right to self-determination for over half a century. He objected to the multilateral discussion of the United States' relationship with Cuba. Nations had the right to determine their own bilateral interests in accordance with their own national values, he said, and that included international relationships.

Many of the nearly 40 speakers throughout the day-long discussion alluded to the sweeping changes—known as the "Arab Spring"—that had recently led thousands of people in the Middle East and North Africa to realize their right to self-determination and to steer the course of their own development. In

light of those "unexpected and profound" political changes, said
the representative of Egypt, speaking on behalf of the Non-Aligned Movement, the application of justice could not be confined
to the national level. It should also extend to the international
arena and to relationships between Member States.

It was "utterly troubling" that, to this day, "the screws of an
unfair and unwarranted blockade . . . are still being tightened"
against Cuba, he said. Nevertheless, the punitive measures
imposed against that country had persisted, "and with them
endures the suffering of its brave people." He urged the United
States to promptly end the embargo and, "once and for all,"
listen to the will of the overwhelming majority of the international community.

Echoing that call, the representative of Saint Vincent and
the Grenadines said that, half a century ago, the world had
witnessed a "Cuban Spring" in the form of an indigenous and
popular uprising against a brutal dictator. They had chosen for
themselves a new path of progress, global citizenship and development which was guided by the fulfilment of the needs of its
citizens, particularly the poor.

Some States had not greeted that uprising with the same
enthusiasm with which they welcomed, assisted or instigated other, subsequent revolutionary movements, the delegate
added. Instead, the embargo imposed on Cuba had been an
"unmitigated failure" and had only caused suffering to its people.
Indeed, while other unjust and antiquated structures had fallen,
it alone remained as the last relic of a Cold War that otherwise
only existed in the history books.

The representative of Vietnam agreed, emphasizing that—
even as the estimated loss and damages caused by the embargo
approached $1 trillion—the suffering of the Cuban people
transcended that "staggering" figure. "The basis of the [embar-
go's] policies and measures is a violation of the right of a people
to self-determination," he stressed, adding that all people had

the right, among other things, to determine their own political system and their path to development.

Also speaking today was the Minister of State for External Affairs of India, as was the Vice Minister for Foreign Affairs of Bolivia.

Representatives of the following countries also spoke: Argentina (on behalf of the Group of 77 developing countries and China), Kenya (on behalf of the African Group), Belize (on behalf of the Caribbean Community/CARICOM), Kazakhstan (on behalf of the Organization of the Islamic Cooperation/ OIC), Uruguay (on behalf of the Southern Common Market/ MERCOSUR), Mexico, Venezuela, China, Algeria, South Africa, Belarus, Indonesia, Solomon Islands, and the Russian Federation.

Also speaking in explanation of the vote before the vote was Nicaragua's delegate.

Speaking in explanation of the vote after the vote were the representatives of Poland (on behalf of the European Union), Namibia, Zambia, Iran, Zimbabwe, Ecuador, Nigeria, Myanmar, Brazil, Syria, Gambia, Sudan, Lao People's Democratic Republic, Saint Kitts and Nevis, Democratic People's Republic of Korea, Argentina, United Republic of Tanzania, and Angola.

The representative of Cuba took the floor in exercise of the right of reply.

The General Assembly will reconvene at 10 a.m. Wednesday, 26 October, to consider the reports of the International Court of Justice and the International Criminal Court.

BACKGROUND

THE GENERAL ASSEMBLY met today to consider the Secretary-General's report on the necessity of ending the economic, commercial and financial embargo imposed by the United States of America against Cuba (document A/66/114), which summarizes the responses of 142 Governments and 26 United Nations bodies, received 11 July 2011, following a request by the Secretary-General on that matter. Replies received after that date will be reproduced in addenda to the present report.

In its 28-page submission for the report, the Cuban Government calls the embargo an act of "genocide," as understood in the Convention for the Prevention and Punishment of the Crime of Genocide, and an act of "economic war" under the terms of the Declaration concerning the laws of naval war, adopted by the Naval Conference of London in 1909. "Despite the official rhetoric that attempts to convince the international public opinion that the current United States Government has introduced positive policy changes, Cuba is still unable to trade with subsidiaries of United States companies in third countries," the Cuban Government states.

"Very conservative estimates" of the direct economic damage to Cubans since December 2010 due to the embargo amounted to $104 billion, Cuba's submission says. That figure would have hit $975 billion if it had accounted for the depreciation of the dollar against the price of gold on the international financial market. The embargo was an "absurd, illegal and morally unsustainable" policy that must be lifted unilaterally, without delay.

DIEGO LIMERES (Argentina), speaking on behalf of the Group of 77 developing countries and China, noted that last year's announcement by the United States on the relaxation of travel restrictions and transfer of remittances had given hope that steps were being taken in the right direction. But a year later, it was clear that those measures had had only limited effect and that the embargo was still in place. Largely unchanged, it continued to impose severe economic and financial restrictions on Cuba that negatively impacted the well-being of its people. Further, it frustrated efforts toward achieving the Millennium Development Goals.

The embargo against Cuba contravened the fundamental norms of international law, international humanitarian law, the United Nations Charter, and the norms and principles governing peaceful relations among States, violating the principles of the sovereign equality of States and of non-intervention and non-interference in each other's domestic affairs, as the Group of 77 and China had pointed out many times before.

At the second South-South Summit in Doha in 2005, the Group had rejected the imposition of laws and regulations with extraterritorial impact and all other forms of coercive economic measures, including unilateral sanctions against developing countries. Recalling that last year a large majority—187 Member States—had voted in favor of the draft resolution presented by Cuba, he said that the Group of 77 and China fully supported the current text calling for an end to the embargo and urged all Member States to do so.

MAGED A. ABDELAZIZ (Egypt), speaking on behalf of the Non-Aligned Movement, recalled that, recently, "unexpected and profound" political changes in many parts of the world had been sparked by an entrenched longing for justice that had, for too long, been unduly denied. In that light, his delegation believed that the application of the principle of justice should not be confined to the national level, but should also extend to the international arena. It should not only govern relations between individuals, but also between Member States. For that reason, it was "utterly troubling" that, to this day, "the screws of an unfair and unwarranted blockade . . . are still being tightened" against one of the Movement's members.

He said that in the past Washington claimed that it would reach out to the Cuban people and engage with them, but such encouraging words had regrettably not been translated into concrete actions. The punitive measures imposed against Cuba had persisted, "and with them endures the suffering of its brave people." The direct and indirect damages caused by the embargo were enormous, affecting all sectors of the economy including health, nutrition, agriculture, banking, trade, investment, and tourism. Moreover, the unilateral blockade had an extended effect on companies and citizens from third countries, thus violating their sovereign rights. The Movement reiterated its deep concern over those harmful impacts, he said, adding that they constituted additional arguments in favor of the prompt elimination of sanctions.

It was astounding that the embargo was maintained when a full 187 Member States had voted last year in favor of the General Assembly resolution that called for its immediate lifting, he said. "Why should the Cuban people continue to suffer when the international community is almost unanimous in its conviction that the cause of their anguish is unjustified and illegal?" he asked, adding that there were no credible answers to that question. The Movement once again urged the United States to immediately and fully comply with all General Assembly resolutions calling for the end of the embargo, and "once and for all" listen to the will of the overwhelming majority of the international community.

MACHARIA KAMAU (Kenya), speaking on behalf of the African Group, said that over the years the General Assembly had categorically and overwhelmingly rejected the imposition of laws and regulations with extraterritorial impact. Africa shared the views expressed by the international community in its continued opposition to sanctions against Cuba. The Assembly called upon all States, in accordance with the United Nations Charter and international law, to refrain from applying, and/or repeal, laws that had extraterritorial impacts affecting the sovereignty of other States, the legitimate interests of entities under their jurisdiction and the freedom of trade and navigation.

Repeated calls by the international community remained unheeded and the "sad and tragic" decades-old United
States embargo on Cuba had remained in force, he said. In
the report of the Secretary-General before the Assembly, the
majority of the United Nations Member States, including
from the African continent and various United Nations entities, categorically rejected the imposition of the embargo on
Cuba and called for its lifting. Given their proximity, Cuba
and the United States should be natural partners in trade,
commerce and investment. Given the large number of Americans of Cuban extraction, Cuba and the United States should
enjoy warm and fraternal relations in social and cultural
affairs among their populations.

Yet the potential of such economic and commercial ties had
sadly remained unrealized, he said, adding: "Whatever the historical roots of this intergenerational embargo, surely the time
has come [for] nations to find the courage and sense of global
citizenry to overcome differences and nurture coexistence." In
conclusion, he reiterated Africa's opposition to unilateral measures that impinged on the sovereignty of another country,
including attempts to extend the application of a country's laws
extraterritorially to other sovereign nations. Africa once again
called for the complete and unequivocal lifting of sanctions and
embargo against Cuba.

JANINE COYE-FELSON (Belize), speaking on behalf of the
Caribbean Community (CARICOM), declared the group's
continued unequivocal opposition to the United States' imposition of the economic, commercial and financial embargo
against Cuba which had been opposed by the overwhelming
majority of the international community for the past 19 consecutive years. The unilateral imposition of extraterritorial laws on
third States was contrary to both the letter and the spirit of the
Charter, and the embargo itself ran counter to the principles of

multilateralism, international law, sovereignty, and free trade that the Organization traditionally championed.

She said the stubborn persistence of the punitive embargo, "apparently impervious to the sustained chorus of international criticism—or logic," was of particular concern to CARICOM, which shared a history, culture, solidarity and kinship with the Cuban people. Noting its regional status as the most populous State of the Caribbean region, and an integral part of the Pan-Caribbean process, she stressed that Caribbean ties with Cuba had historical significance, cemented by years of active cooperation at various levels, including in the areas of trade, health care, infrastructure, and human resource development.

Continuing, she said the significance of the embargo on the Cuban economy continued to be of great concern to CARICOM, and its humanitarian impact on the Cuban people, especially in the health care and food areas, was particularly saddening. The inability of Cuba to acquire much-needed medical equipment, spare parts, and latest-generation medications because of the embargo continued to affect adversely the island nation's health care system. The situation had not been made any easier by the strengthening and more frequent storms and hurricanes wrought by climate change and Cuba's geographical susceptibility to those natural disasters. Given Cuba's peaceful, generous and cooperative international stance, CARICOM reiterated its support for the right of the Cuban people to self-determination, in a manner beneficial to their social and economic development. She remained hopeful, however, that the United States' recent recommitment to multilateralism would result in an increased willingness to consider the opinions and concerns of its global friends and partners on that issue.

BYRGANYM AITIMOVA (Kazakhstan), speaking on behalf of the Council of Ministers of the Organization of Islamic Cooperation (OIC), said that her delegation stood for the rights of every nation to follow its own development, and in that context, condemned unilateral acts that affected sovereignty and State interests. "We do not agree with any national regulations that infringe, impede or retard the development of any country, including [in the] economic, commercial and financial spheres," she said, underlining that the imposition of arbitrary unilateral laws contradicted World Trade Organization (WTO) rules prohibiting measures that hindered free trade and shipping. Like the "overwhelming majority" of the international community, she called for lifting the Cuban embargo in line with the United Nations Charter and General Assembly resolutions.

JOSÉ LUIS CANCELA (Uruguay), speaking on behalf of the Southern Common Market (MERCOSUR), regretted that the "blockade policy" against Cuba continued unchanged, and had in fact recorded an increase in the restrictions to Cuba's financial transactions with third countries, and that conditions were again obstructing the way of a greater openness to a direct dialogue. MERCOSUR and its Associated States believed that the embargo against Cuba went against the principles of the Charter and contradicted the rules of international law, mainly the equality of States, non-intervention in domestic affairs, peaceful settlement of disputes, as well as the rules of the multilateral trade system and those that obliged the members of the WTO.

He said the embargo, which was also against the principles of justice and human rights, represented a collective punishment, created shortages and suffering to the population, limited and delayed development, and seriously harmed the Cuban economy. Thus, as a matter of principle, MERCOSUR rejected unilateral and extraterritorial measures and in that sense, condemned the application of coercive unilateral measures against free trade, which caused an irremediable damage to the people's welfare and obstructed the process of regional integration. The economic, commercial, and financial embargo imposed against Cuba was an example of obsolete policies that did not have a place in today's world, he added.

H. E. AHAMED (Minister of State for External Affairs of India), aligning with the Group of 77 and China, as well as the Non-Aligned Movement, said the Assembly had repeatedly rejected the imposition of laws with extraterritorial impact and all other forms of coercive economic measures. It also had called on States to respect the Charter and international law yet despite that, the United States' embargo against Cuba remained in full force, which severely undermined the credibility of the United Nations. Indeed, the embargo had brought immense suffering for Cubans and had transgressed a sovereign State's right to development.

Moreover, it had adversely affected Cuba's economic prosperity, he said, by denying it access to the United States' market, investment, technology and financial services, as well as to scientific, educational, cultural and sporting institutions. The embargo's extraterritorial application also had severely impacted health care, a Millennium Development Goal, as well as health assistance to developing countries. There was huge potential to strengthen economic and commercial ties. Steps taken this year by the United States to reduce restrictions on travel and remittances were positive developments, but they were far from enough to make a fundamental change. India joined others in calling for an immediate end to the Cuban embargo. He supported the resolution.

JUAN CARLOS ALURRALDE (Bolivia) said that the Cold War fear of nuclear attacks had largely ended, but other issues—including the threat of climate change—"now strike fear in our hearts." He called on the United States to recall the time of John F. Kennedy, in which an American President had supported the right of the German people to determine their own fate and development. Indeed, today's United States President should say "I am Cuban," in the way that Kennedy had declared "I am a Berliner."

Those that claimed to support democracy were denying the right to democracy in the Assembly Hall today, he continued. How long would the world wait for that State to change its attitude? It was crucial that the United States adhere to the wishes of the vast majority of those in the room. For those reasons, among others, Bolivia fully supported the draft resolution currently before the Assembly.

LUIS-ALFONSO DE ALBA (Mexico) said that the draft resolution before the Assembly reflected, for the twentieth consecutive year, the international community's rejection of the embargo imposed against Cuba. Mexico was opposed to the use of coercive measures that ran counter to the principles of international law, as well as those of the Charter. That blockade blatantly contradicted negotiations, diplomacy and dialogue as ways to resolve disputes between States. Many United Nations agencies and bodies, alongside the report currently before the Assembly, had highlighted the negative effects of he embargo—both those that directly affected the Cuban people and those which had an indirect impact on third party States.

For those reasons, Mexico had supported all resolutions against the United States' unilateral measures. It continued to support the inclusion of Cuba in dialogue on economic, financial, and commercial matters at the international level. Mexico's geographical proximity helped it to understand the plight of Cuba. Additionally, Mexico felt strongly that multilateralism remained the best way to resolve disputes and to ensure peaceful coexistence between States. Once again, the near-universal rejection of the embargo showed that the time was ripe for lifting that blockade.

JORGE VALERO (Venezuela) endorsed the statements by the representatives of Egypt on behalf of the Non-Aligned Movement, Argentina on behalf of the Group of 77 and China, and Uruguay on behalf of the Southern Common Market (MERCOSUR). He echoed the fact that Member States had made a near-universal call from the Assembly to end the embargo against Cuba, which, for more than 50 years, had sought to restrict the right of that country's people to decide their own fate. That was an "unequivocal sign" that it was necessary to defend the political independence of States, and the fundamental purposes of the United Nations. It was shameful that the call was ignored year after year.

In that regard, Venezuela supported the various statements on Cuba that had been approved by several groups and forums worldwide. It was important to remember that a number of Cuban citizens—namely Gerardo Hernandez, Ramon Labañino, Antonio Guerrerro, and Fernando Gonzalez Llort—remained detained in the United States for defending their homeland against terrorist attacks. It was also necessary to remember Rene Gonzalez, who had been released but was forced to remain in the United States. Under the embargo, legislation such as the Torricelli Act and the Helms-Burton Act restricted trade and imposed restrictions against entrepreneurs who wished to invest in Cuba.

However, the blockade was not an "abstract device imposed against a government," but had a daily impact on the lives of women, men and children. It negatively affected the quality of life of sick people, who were denied medical items whose sale was prohibited in Cuba. It prevented the import of building materials that were needed to make repairs. Despite those challenges, Cuba had sustained a generous amount of support to neighboring and other countries. For those reasons, he demanded the end to the blockade and to the imposition of international double standards. "Let us stop allowing the condemnation of the weak," he stressed, "and the toleration of violations committed by the imperialists of the North."

WANG MIN (China) said that for nineteen years, the Assembly had adopted, by an overwhelming majority, resolutions on the need to end the Cuban embargo, urging all countries to abide by the Charter and international law, and to repeal measures with extraterritorial effect. Regrettably, those texts had not been implemented and the Cuban embargo had yet to be lifted, which severely violated the Charter and inflicted enormous economic and financial loss on Cuba. The embargo had impeded efforts to eradicate poverty and violated Cubans' basic human rights to food, health, and education.

China had always believed that countries should develop mutual relations on the basis of upholding the Charter and respecting the right of others to choose their development paths, he said, adding that China opposed unilateral sanctions imposed by military, political, economic or other means. Noting that China and Cuba had maintained "normal" economic, trade and personal exchanges, he said such mutually beneficial cooperation continued to grow. Dialogue and harmonious coexistence were the mainstream of international relations, and in that context he hoped the United States would follow the tenets of the Charter and end its embargo as soon as possible. He also hoped the relationship between the United States and Cuba would improve with a view to promoting regional development. China would support today's resolution.

MOURAD BENMEHIDI (Algeria) said the consecutive annual adoption by an overwhelming majority of Assembly members of a similar resolution calling for the lifting of the embargo against Cuba reflected the profound wish of the international community to put an end to that situation, which had lasted far too long. Algeria had always condemned the imposition of unilateral acts, extraterritorial regulations impeding the development of any country and all forms of coercive economic and trade measures, such as the economic, commercial and financial embargo against Cuba, which was openly contrary to international law and the purposes and principles of the Charter. Every Member State should respect principles of the Charter, including the sovereign equality of States, territorial integrity and non-intervention in the internal affairs of any other State. It was well established that this blockade affected Cuba's economic growth and impeded its human development.

In that regard, it had caused huge economic damage to Cuba, and created economic hardship, daily affecting the well-being of the Cuban people. Those consequences were exacerbated by the adverse effects of the current global and financial crisis, and the energy and food crisis that had seriously compromised Cuba's efforts to improve its level of development. According to estimates by the Cuban Government, confirmed by the United Nations Development Program (UNDP), the cumulative direct and indirect losses to the Cuban economy over 50 years were more than $100 billion. In accordance with the long-standing position of the Non-Aligned Movement on the issue, Algeria rejected the use of economic measures of coercion and extraterritorial applications of laws imposed on developing countries, and urged the United States Government to end the embargo against Cuba.

DOCTOR MASHABANE (South Africa) said the question of ending the embargo against Cuba had continued to be a problem for the United Nations despite many calls to eliminate the measures. The time had come for the embargo to be lifted, and the people of Cuba continued to bear the brunt of the sanctions. The blockade was a violation of the sovereign equality of States, non-intervention and non-interference in domestic affairs. It was a violation of international law and showed disregard of the United Nations Charter. Thus South Africa joined the majority of countries expressing opposition to all aspects of the blockade. The situation was further exacerbated by the global financial crisis, food crisis, and climate change. The embargo directly hindered the Cuban economic recovery, and negatively impacted tourism. The damage was estimated to exceed $975 billion in the future. South Africa rejected reinforcement of the sanctions.

South Africa was deeply concerned over the widening of the extraterritorial nature of the embargo and rejected the reinforcement of the measures aimed at tightening it, as well as all other recent measures carried out by the United States against Cuba. His delegation condemned the seizing by the United States of over $4.2 million, in January 2011, of funding from the Global Fund to Fight AIDS, Tuberculosis and Malaria, which had been earmarked for the implementation of cooperation projects with Cuba. He supported the content of the press release of 18 October 2011 by the Permanent Mission of the Republic of Cuba to the United Nations concerning the intensification of sanctions and extraterritorial persecution of citizens, institutions, and companies in third countries that established economic, commercial, financial, scientific and technical ties with Cuba.

South Africa was strongly opposed to the actions of the United States regarding fines levied against foreign banking institutions for having conducted operations with Cuba. In an attempt to grow trade with Cuba, South Africa was finalizing its proposals to offer a credit line of $10 million to Cuba. That would be a breakthrough in relations for trade cooperation. He called on all Member States to support the lifting of the United States' embargo against Cuba.

LE HOAI TRUNG (Vietnam) recalled that, by the end of the current meeting, the Assembly would have overwhelmingly adopted for 20 consecutive years a resolution on the issue of ending the Cuban embargo. Vietnam shared the view of the international community that the United States should end the embargo against Cuba, which is a peace-loving nation, for strong legal, political, economic and humanitarian reasons. The General Assembly had reaffirmed that the policies and measures in pursuit of the embargo, including the Helms-Burton Act, went against international law and the purposes and principles of the United Nations Charter. "The basis of these policies and measures is a violation of the right of a people to self-determination," he stressed, adding that they had the right, among other things, to determine their political system and path of development.

Additionally, he said, the embargo had serious and illegal extraterritorial effects on the sovereignty of other States, the legitimate interests of persons under their jurisdiction, their freedom of trade and navigation. The Government of Cuba estimated that the loss and damages caused by the embargo amounted to nearly $1 trillion. The suffering of the Cuban people, however, transcended that "staggering figure." For those reasons, Heads of State or Government had reiterated their call to end the embargo in the Outcome Document of the fifteenth Non-Aligned Summit held in Egypt in 2009, he said. Similarly, the discussions taking place today were consistent with the urge for cooperation and dialogue and the General Assembly's current theme of peaceful settlement of disputes.

CAMILLO M. GONSALVES (St. Vincent and the Grenadines) said that "half a century ago, the world was witness to the 'Cuban Spring': an indigenous and popular uprising against a corrupt and brutal dictator." The Cuban people, unassisted by foreign military forces, had cast off the shackles of rapacious exploitation and chose for themselves a new and uniquely adapted path of progress, global citizenship, and development that was measured not by the levels of corporate or individual excess, but on the fulfillment of the needs of its citizens, particularly the poor.

Some States had not greeted that "Cuban Spring" with the same enthusiasm with which they welcomed, assisted or instigated other, subsequent revolutionary movements.

Noting that the scale and scope of the Cuban embargo had no parallel in the modern world, he aligned with those calling for it to end. He said no one in the Assembly Hall had the right to tell the United States how to conduct its foreign policy or who its friends should be. At the same time, all Member States were obliged to uphold the Charter and reject instances where national foreign policy decisions "morphed into violations of international law."

The embargo had been an "unmitigated failure" and had only caused suffering for the Cuban people. While other unjust and antiquated structures had fallen, it alone remained as the last relic of a Cold War that otherwise only existed in the history books. "In an interconnected world of open borders, free movement of people, goods and capital, how can the architects of globalization simultaneously legislate the isolation of one State, or place extraterritorial restrictions on commerce, global trade and the movement of individuals?" he asked. Citing President Obama's inaugural address to the Assembly on demonstrating that international law was not an empty promise, he urged him to heed the overwhelming voice of the international community.

NIKOLAI OVSYANKO (Belarus) said that the overwhelming majority of Member States had been demanding the end of the economic, commercial and financial embargo against Cuba for decades, regarding it as an uncivilized and unconstructive means of resolving international disagreements. Unilateral sanctions negatively impacted the lives of the Cuban people, particularly given the economic and financial crises in the world today, which appeared to be about to embark on a second wave.

Noting that the blockade contradicted international law and United Nations decisions, he said that in the current system of international relations, there was no place for unilateral sanctions or other unilateral economic measures to pressure sovereign States. Nations had the right to determine their own developmental paths. He hoped that the voice of the General Assembly would be heard as it passed the resolution for the twentieth time.

YUSRA KHAN (Indonesia) called for the conclusion of the unilateral economic, commercial and financial embargo imposed against Cuba. The measures undermined the principles of the Charter and of international law, as well as the rights of people to life, well-being and development. In addition, although imposed unilaterally, the embargo impacted the economic and commercial interests and relations of third countries. It had also severely affected the daily welfare of Cuban citizens and posed an unnecessary burden to the attainment of the Millennium Development Goals.

Since the embargo had initially been imposed, much had changed, he continued. Globalization had created conditions for true global solidarity and partnership among nations. Lifting the embargo would be in keeping with the spirit of the times. "The time is ripe for relations between the two main parties to be transformed through constructive engagement," he said. While encouraged by the small, but meaningful, changes that had recently occurred, including the easing of travel restrictions to Cuba and the removal of obstacles to transfer of remittances, he called on all countries to adhere to the principles of equality, mutual respect, peaceful coexistence and good-neighborliness and respect for human rights.

COLLIN BECK (Solomon Islands), associating himself with the statement of the Group of 77 and China, said that his delegation would again vote with the majority of United Nations Members in support of the resolution to end the blockade against

Cuba. He asked the United States, which had "absolute power" within the multilateral system, to examine its actions toward the people of Cuba through the lens of humanity and to renew its friendship with that country.

In a changing world, the rights, freedoms, and laws that were frequently spoken of should be upheld with respect for States to adopt their own political systems, he said. As a small island developing country, Solomon Islands believed in multilateralism and would vote in support of the resolution.

VITALY I. CHURKIN (Russian Federation) said his country's position on the resolution was well known and remained unchanged: "We express total solidarity with the overwhelming majority of members of the international community who are strongly condemning the trade and economic embargo against Cuba." The anti-Cuba blockade had lasted almost half a century and had clearly been unable to influence Cuba's sovereign choice of development model. The only consequences of the sanctions had been deteriorated living standards for Cubans, artificial barriers to economic growth and infringements on third-country interests.

The United States' unilateral, restrictive actions against Cuba had only created the opposite effect of what their instigators had intended during the Cold War, he said, adding that the current United States Administration had raised expectations about changes to Washington's policy but had made only minimum steps. He hoped the United States' decision to end restrictions on visits by United States citizens to family in Cuba as well as on remittances and postal orders would be followed by steps to normalize relations with Cuba and to lift the embargo. His Government strongly believed such moves would foster progressive social and economic reforms by the Cuban leadership. The Russian Federation would vote in favor of today's text.

INTRODUCTION AND ACTION ON DRAFT

BRUNO EDUARDO RODRIGUEZ PARRILLA, Minister for Foreign Affairs of Cuba, introduced the draft on the "necessity of ending the economic, commercial and financial embargo imposed by the United States of America against Cuba." He said that through the Torricelli Act—the official action that had led to the "notorious" extraterritorial implementation of the blockade laws against third States—the United States had committed to strengthening the siege around the island of Cuba in a cruelly opportunistic manner.

The General Assembly had adopted the decision to include the current item in its agenda in 1991, he recalled, and at that time, it had seemed impossible that the Assembly would still be discussing the matter 20 years later. Indeed, for two decades, the Assembly had invariably called for an end to the economic, commercial, and financial blockade by the United States. In 1996, the Helms-Burton Act had expanded the unprecedented extraterritorial scope of the blockade and comprehensively typified the "change of regime" and eventual intervention in Cuba; no one knew if the "Bush Plan for Cuba" of 2004 had been abrogated.

The direct economic damage imposed exceeded $975 billion, he said, adding that the United States Government, in a 1960 referendum, had itself stated that the objectives pursued by the blockade had been to cause "disenchantment and disaffection based on economic dissatisfaction and hardship . . . to weaken the economic life of Cuba, to decrease monetary and real wages, to bring about hunger, desperation and to overthrow the Government." Today, Cuba was still unable to freely export or import products or services of any sort to and from the United States, to use American dollars, or other restrictions.

He said that the ban on Cuban companies' trade with American subsidiaries in third countries also remained unchanged, while entrepreneurs interested in investing in Cuba continued to be sanctioned, threatened, or blacklisted. In January 2011, more than $4 million in financing from the Global Fund to Fight AIDS, Tuberculosis, and Malaria—which was destined to fund projects in Cuba—had been confiscated; meanwhile, while there had been an "alleged" relaxation of laws preventing Americans from traveling to Cuba, the truth was that freedom of travel continued to be hampered.

Pointing out a number of other examples of the negative effects of the embargo—which, he stressed, were "endless"—he recalled that President Obama had recently responded with a "noncommittal refusal" to an offer made by the Cuban Government to hold a dialogue on items on the bilateral agenda. For its part, Cuba was changing its will, aiming for "more revolution and a better socialism." Indeed, the only thing that had not changed in the last 50 years had been the blockade and the "hostile and aggressive policy of the United States." Cuba would continue to promote equal opportunities for every child and would not abandon anyone to his or her own fate. It would not renounce social programs, nor universal health and education. It would continue to guarantee the right to work, the right to equal pay, and other rights. "We will continue to believe in human values," he said, adding that all Cuban citizens would continue to be able to exercise their human rights.

Family ties and the limited cultural, academic, and scientific exchange that currently existed between the United States and Cuba showed how positive it would be to expand those links for the benefit of both peoples. Cuba's proposal to move toward normalization of relations and to expand bilateral cooperation in different areas still stood, he stressed, adding nonetheless that the five Cuban political prisoners serving unjust sentences in the United States or forbidden to return to Cuba must be released. He further asked the community of nations to support the draft resolution currently before the Assembly.

Speaking in explanation of position before action on the text, the representative of the United States said that the draft resolution had been designed to "confuse and obscure." The United States reaffirmed its strong commitment to the right of the Cuban people to fully determine their own future, he stressed, adding that in fact the Cuban regime had denied them of that right for more than half a century. The United States further affirmed its right to determine its own bilateral interests in accordance with its own national values, and that included international relationships. In that regard, its relationship with Cuba—of which the embargo was only one part—was a bilateral issue and a matter of national concern.

Indeed, the annual exercise by the Assembly attempted, "to no good end," to obscure some fundamental truths. The Cuban Government's own policy was the largest obstacle to the country's own development, concentrating political and economic decisions in the hands of the few and stifling economic growth. The exercise further concealed the fact that the United States was a leading source of food and humanitarian aid to Cuba, and that it did not restrict aid to that country. In 2010 alone, Cuba had received $3.5 billion in total sales of United States goods, including some $360 million in agricultural products. It had also authorized $861 million in humanitarian assistance to Cuba. Those figures alone were enough to rebut the "spurious allegations of genocide," he stressed, adding that the charge greatly misused that important term and insulted its true victims.

Moreover, the draft and the "stale rhetoric around it" ignored some basic facts. The United States was, in fact, open to a new relationship with Cuba, which could begin if the Cuban Government began to respect human rights and the rights of Cuban citizens to determine their own destiny. Cuba should also release American citizen Alan Gross, who had been sentenced to 15 years in prison for trying to connect the Cuban

Jewish population to the Internet. Recent changes in policy, made by President Obama, built upon the country's previous engagement with Cuba, and showed the strong commitment of the United States to the Cuban people—contrary to the picture that had been painted throughout the current debate.

The United States was prepared to do its part, but improving the situation required efforts by the Cuban Government as well. It must ensure that the Cuban people enjoyed the freedoms on which the United Nations insisted in the cases of other countries, he stressed. For those reasons, and because the resolution did not reflect current realities, the United States would vote against it.

Also speaking ahead of the vote, the representative of Nicaragua said the General Assembly would again demand an end to the embargo toward the Cuban people, and the United States was trying to justify and bend a people who would never bend, because they had a will of steel. He made clear his support of the resolution, and expressed support regarding the updated information on the damages the United States was causing to Cuba with the most criminal embargo in the history of mankind. He recognized Cuba's generosity and humanism, and said who if not Cuba was the first to step up when its neighbors were in need.

However, he said there was an attempt to destroy the Cuban socialist revolution by continuing to implement the embargo, and it must end now. It had been clearly shown that nobody supported the embargo and it was time to correct the measures that violated humanitarian law and the United Nations Charter. Even the people of the United States did not support this embargo and more voices were calling for an end to this inhumane policy.

He said that regional Governments, who along with Cuba tenaciously fought the embargo, considered blockade a policy of intervention in the region. He said that the region would walk hand in hand until "this historic error" was made right. He noted that the policy was an obstacle to Cuba's development and called for its end. Indeed, nobody was fooled "by more than 50 years of terrorist acts." One gesture would be to free the Cuban heroic patriots in prison, as they defended Cuba. Once again, he expressed his strongest condemnation of this embargo, which was contrary to international law and a threat to peace and multilateralism, and an insult to human values.

The Assembly then adopted the resolution on ending the embargo imposed by the United States against Cuba (document A/66/L.4) by a recorded vote of 186 in favor to 2 against (United States, Israel) with 3 abstentions (Marshall Islands, Palau, Micronesia).

Explanations of Vote After the Vote

The representative of Poland, speaking on behalf of the European Union and associated countries, said his delegation opposed extraterritorial measures taken in United States law, such as the Helms-Burton and Torricelli Acts. Those measures must not be allowed to affect commercial relations between Cuba and EU member States. The European Union's position regarding relations with Cuba had been set out in 1996 and reflected a common position. He sought a result-oriented engagement with Cuba and reaffirmed the EU's commitment to continuing dialogue with the Cuban Government, civil society and other actors.

Reiterating the right of the Cuban people to decide their own future, he welcomed the Cuban Government's release of 75 political prisoners, and called upon it to recognize the civil and political rights of its people and to accede to the International Covenants on Civil and Political Rights and on Economic, Social and Cultural Rights. Noting the negative impact of the embargo on the Cuban people, he rejected all unilateral measures against Cuba that were contrary to international law. The European Union had unanimously voted in favor of the resolution.

Namibia's representative said that this year marked the twentieth anniversary the Assembly had acted on a similar resolution on the embargo, but the blockade was still in place. That was in stark contrast to the overwhelming appeal by the international community to end this unjust policy against the people of Cuba. In fact, the debate would not have been necessary had the United States lifted the blockade years ago. His delegation voted in favor of the draft resolution because he believed in the principle of peaceful coexistence of all nations, respect for sovereign equality, open trade among nations, and above all, the spirit of good neighborliness.

The imposition of the blockade against Cuba was an outdated form of punishment. His delegation remained concerned about the promulgation and application of laws and measures constituting economic embargo against any friendly and peaceful country. He said that Namibia had always maintained the view that the blockade ran counter to the spirit of the United Nations Charter, international law and the Millennium Declaration. The same blockade continued to cause irreparable damage to the economic, social, and cultural development of Cuba as it deprived its people of the opportunities emanating from free trade.

The Torricelli and Helms-Burton Acts were extraterritorial in nature and thus interfered with the sovereign rights of Cuba and violated the rules of international trading systems. He was convinced that the two neighboring countries would both benefit from the normalization of relations and the removal of restrictions between them. "In our view, all human rights, be they political, cultural, or economic, are inseparable. Through the blockade, the people of Cuba are being denied these basic fundamental human rights just because of the political system they have chosen," he said. Thus, Namibia voted in favor of the draft resolution, and expressed solidarity with the people of Cuba.

Also speaking in explanation of vote, the representative of Zambia said the Assembly found itself in a situation that reminded his delegation of "Humpty Dumpty" who said that "words only mean that which I want them to." As such, he asked what democracy was if the universal resolutions of the United Nations that called for the lifting of sanctions are routinely ignored.

"What is the rule of law if General Assembly resolutions that declare sanctions illegal continue to be ignored?" and "Is the law only a law when [one] decides it is a law?" When the international community talked about sovereign equality of nations, did that principle only apply when it concerned the sovereignty of "someone we like"? It was thought that true freedom embraced a diversity of opinion, thought, and political systems. Indeed freedom also meant the right to be wrong. He said his delegation voted in favor of the resolution because "it is the right thing to do."

The representative of Iran said that the overwhelming support for the resolution reflected the common understanding and will of the international community concerning the "inhumane and illegitimate" embargo imposed by the United States against the Cuban Government and people. Depriving civilian populations of their economic and social rights infringed upon their basic human rights and was therefore illegal. Indeed, this was the main feature of the sanctions as known today. Such measures were illegal largely because economic sanctions were a tool to impose hegemonic intentions of big powers; sanctions always ended in targeting daily lives of civilians; sanctions had proven to be futile and there was no strong proof that independent nations compromised their revered national interests to hegemonic powers due to sanctions.

The most deplorable form of sanctions was the imposition of unilateral blockades and extraterritorial application of domestic laws by one State. Numerous international documents had called for swift invalidation of all such measures. Indeed, one wondered what more should be done to convince the Government of the United States to lift the inhumane and futile economic blockade. He said his delegation strongly rejected and remained opposed to the application of unilateral and economic trade measures by one State against another, as well as to the extraterritorial application and effects of national legislation on the sovereignty of other States.

The representative of Zimbabwe said the last 20 years had heard an overwhelming number of States call for the end of the Cuban embargo, a blockade which violated international law and countered the United Nations Charter, to which the United States was a founding signatory. It also frustrated Cuba's efforts to reach the Millennium Development Goals and denied the country access to markets, development aid, and technology transfer, all of which were vital to its development. Zimbabwe understood the difficulties associated with such ill-conceived measures, as it also had fallen victim to them. Her Government rejected the passage of laws with the goal of achieving regime change. Cuban national pride had taken root to defeat such foreign interference. She expressed solidarity with the Government and people of Cuba and had voted in favor of today's text.

The representative of Ecuador congratulated Cuba on today's victory. Ecuador had voted in favor of the resolution which was counter to international law and the principles of peaceful interaction among States. The blockade jeopardized the Cuban people. He demanded an end to the blockade and all unilateral actions counter to international law and appealed to common sense to end the blockade.

The representative of Nigeria, aligning with the Group of 77 and China, as well as the Non-Aligned Movement, supported States' inalienable right to determine their own development model. Nigeria was "uncomfortable" with the embargo against

Cuba, as it countered multilateralism, international law, soverei-gnty, and free trade, principles the Assembly had championed for years. Nigeria opposed the punishment of innocent people and, thus, favored the dismantling of both the structures that enforced the embargo and the logic underpinning its existence. For such reasons, Nigeria had voted in favor of the resolution.

Also speaking in explanation of vote after the vote, the representative of Myanmar said that his delegation sup-ported Cuba, particularly regarding the situation of that country's elderly, women and children. The hardships set in motion by the embargo affected the innocent people of Cuba, and went against the sovereign equality outlined in the United Nations Charter. Moreover, the measures deviated from international law.

Brazil's speaker said that the economic, financial and social blockade against Cuba had been rejected by the great majority of Member States, including his own country, for the twentieth time in as many years. It went against international law and inhibited regional relations. Although measures announced by Washington last January had been positive, they did not change the situation or mitigate the suffering of the Cuban people. Brazil had voted in favor of the resolution.

Syria's representative said the Cuban embargo contravened the principles of international law, including humanitarian law, the sovereign equality between States, non-intervention and freedom of navigation and trade. It was illegal and challenged the legal credibility of United States' policies. Such measures had been imposed by the United States and other European countries with the goal of weakening some States, attempting to force them to adopt certain measures or change their policies.

He said the embargo had caused more than $10 billion in damage to the Cuban economy and violated human rights. Despite that the Assembly had issued resolutions for 20 years, the embargo remained. Sanctions imposed on developing countries, including Syria, constituted collective punishment under the pretext of maintaining human rights. He called for ending the embargo and hostile policies pursued outside the framework of international law. For such reasons, Syria voted in favor of the resolution.

In explanation of the vote, the representative of Gambia said in light of the global economic crisis, this was neither the time nor the season to impose sanctions or reinforce them. Even in the best of times, they inflicted untold suffering. As the global financial crisis continued unabated all nations were under constant pressure from the negative impact of the crisis. The economic embargo could be characterized as "aggression" against a sovereign State, with a negative downstream effect, particularly on vulnerable groups.

Many delegations pointed out that the sanctions undermined the capacity of Cuba to obtain the Millennium Development Goals. In light of all that, Gambia was consistent in its support of denouncing the sanctions and calling for the repeal of laws relating to Cuba. Gambia had supported the resolution of this august body, out of the necessity of ending the sanctions. In conclusion, she aligned herself with the statements made by the Group of 77, the Non-Aligned Movement, the African States and the Organization of Islamic Cooperation.

Sudan's representative said that the international community had rejected unilateral coercive measures that crossed borders. Continued support for the resolution revealed "total rejection" of the embargo, as it violated the basic principles of the Charter, international law and norms governing national economic and commercial relations between States, and inhibited development. Since 1997, Sudan too had suffered from such unilateral measures by the United States with deleterious effect on the people's well-being. He condemned the imposition of such measures on developing countries and called for a world where all States lived in peace. That required commitment to the

Charter's principles and to sound management of international relations. He urged States that had taken unilateral measures against other States to repeal them.

The representative of Lao People's Democratic Republic said that for the twentieth consecutive year, the Assembly had adopted, by an overwhelming majority, a resolution demanding an end to the embargo against Cuba, and called on all States to respect the Charter and norms of international law. It also called for an end to all measures whose extraterritorial effects threatened the sovereignty of States or the legitimate interests of persons under their jurisdiction.

Despite such calls, the embargo and its extraterritorial aspects seriously violated the goals and principles of the Charter and relevant United Nations resolutions, he said, which had caused considerable economic losses for Cubans. The embargo also had impeded efforts to eliminate poverty, promote economic and social development and attain the Millennium Development Goals. Reiterating his opposition to the embargo, he reaffirmed his country's solidarity with the Cuban people and joined international calls to end the embargo.

The representative of Saint Kitts and Nevis voted in favor of today's text and said that Cuba was among his country's closest allies. Saint Kitts and Nevis also respected the United States' role in international relations and recognized its recent concessions related to the embargo. "However, that is not enough. Friends must tell friends when they are wrong or misguided," he said. In supporting the resolution, his country continued to be an advocate of that truth.

Supporting the principles of sovereignty, non-intervention, and the strengthened role of the United Nations in international affairs, he said Saint Kitts and Nevis did not support measures that impeded free trade. Nor did it apply laws that had extraterritorial effect. It felt strongly about ending the Cuban embargo. Cuba was a pan-Caribbean partner, and the embargo's negative impact on it was "profound and unfair." Amid a global recession, the embargo stunted Cuba's development, which contravened the principles held dear by those imposing it. It also impeded progress, which was why he had voted in favor of today's resolution and called on both sides to find common ground.

The representative of the Democratic People's Republic of Korea said that today was the twentieth year the topic was being debated. In addition, for many decades, major documents had been adopted at international and regional meetings on the issue, and there were more calls than ever to end the blockade against Cuba. Yet, those sanctions remained in place a full decade into the new century. The embargo was aimed at destroying the socialist system, even though the Cuban people had chosen that system freely.

The Democratic People's Republic of Korea condemned strongly the economic embargo as it violated the Charter and had been "flagrantly imposed" on the sovereignty of Cuba and its people. Once again, he urged the United States to lift the economic, commercial and financial embargo at the soonest possible time. Finally, he expressed support and solidarity with the Cuban people to preserve their sovereignty in the face of the embargo.

Argentina's representative said his country had voted in favor of the resolution and would fully implement it. Foreign laws were not valid when they claimed to have extraterritorial effect, including through extending an economic blockade with the goal of changing a Government. His delegation's vote today reflected a position that favored an end to unilateral measures and a commitment to multilateralism. The Cuban embargo countered the principles of international law and the United Nations Charter. It endured, despite the numerous international calls against it. Rejecting the embargo, he reiterated his firm support for Cuba.

The representative of the United Republic of Tanzania, aligning with the statement made on behalf of the Group of 77 and China, and with the Non-Aligned Movement, said that, as in past years, his delegation had voted against the embargo for the Cuban people who had suffered so long under it. Despite the call for the embargo's end, the people of Cuba continued to suffer as though the international community did not care.

"Whenever the bulls fight, it's the grass which gets hurt," he said, reciting an adage from his country which adequately reflected the adverse effect on common people of any embargo, he said. It was high time to end the suffering once and for all. Despite encouraging measures taken by the United States since 2009, the embargo continued to severely constrain Cuba's development and improvement of the standard of living of its citizens. He supported direct dialogue between the parties to resolve their differences for the betterment of Cuba's citizens.

The representative of Angola said the Assembly had once again adopted a resolution urging all countries to withdraw laws and regulations with extraterritorial measures that under-mined State sovereignty. He was perplexed as to why the United States embargo against Cuba remained in place, as it violated State sovereignty and encroached on the rights of persons, entities and companies under State jurisdiction to establish or propose economic, commercial, financial or scientific relations with Cuba. He urged international support for more engage-ment between the two countries, with a view to identifying a solution.

He went on to say that the Secretary-General's report stated there had been no improvement toward ending the embargo, a measure that had severely penalized Cubans by preventing economic programs from being carried out. Angola adhered to the Charter and respected all Assembly resolutions, he said, rei-terating his country's commitment to international law, which supported the elimination of all coercive economic measures as a means of political persuasion. Angola had voted in favor of the resolution, as the embargo flagrantly violated the right to sovereignty and equality among States, as well as the principle of non-interference in the internal affairs of other States.

RIGHT OF REPLY

EXERCISING HIS DELEGATION'S right of reply, Cuba's speaker said he was taking the floor to counter the "flagrant lies" by the United States delegate in defense of the policies of former President George W. Bush and President Barack Obama. He agreed that the blockade was just "one facet" of the United States' policy against Cuba. Other acts included subversion, the deployment of agents on Cuban territory and CIA covert operations. He would ensure that the Geneva Convention on Genocide reached the United States' delegate's desk, as his country was responsible for extrajudicial executions, torture, kidnapping, and use of secret jails in Europe. The United States even maintained a "concentration camp" on illegally occupied land in Guantánamo.

There were strict relations between the two countries that could not be described as trade relations, he said, because provisions in the international trade system were routinely flouted. The United States' delegate also had lied when he cited humanitarian aid provided by the United States Agency for International Development (USAID). Rather than wage wars, the United States would do better to heed the voice of its own people, notably those down in Wall Street, who were complaining about an absence of true democracy in the United States, about corporations that placed profit before people, and about the triumph of egoism over justice. People were complaining they had lost their homes, lost pensions, and lost social security while the rich received bonuses.

He went on to say that more than 3,000 United States citizens were now on death row, adding that just a few weeks ago, the world had watched aghast as Troy Davis had been executed. While the United States delegate had said a United States citizen was being held in Cuba for connecting the Jewish community to the Internet, he also understood that that person had committed a crime that was subject to sanctions in the United States. Moreover, the five Cubans suffering under cruel and degrading conditions for trying to avert terrorist acts against the United States should be freed. The political battle being waged today was for an end to the Cuban blockade and a system that engendered injustice, he said.

Vote on Ending U.S. Embargo against Cuba

THE DRAFT RESOLUTION on the Necessity of Ending the Economic, Commercial and Financial Embargo Imposed by the United States Against Cuba (document A/66/L.4) was adopted by a recorded vote of 186 in favor to 2 against, with 3 abstentions, as follows:

IN FAVOR: Afghanistan, Albania, Algeria, Andorra, Angola, Antigua and Barbuda, Argentina, Armenia, Australia, Austria, Azerbaijan, Bahamas, Bahrain, Bangladesh, Barbados, Belarus, Belgium, Belize, Benin, Bhutan, Bolivia, Bosnia and Herzegovina, Botswana, Brazil, Brunei Darussalam, Bulgaria, Burkina Faso, Burundi, Cambodia, Cameroon, Canada, Cape Verde, Central African Republic, Chad, Chile, China, Colombia, Comoros, Congo, Costa Rica, Côte d'Ivoire, Croatia, Cuba, Cyprus, Czech Republic, Democratic People's Republic of Korea, Democratic Republic of the Congo, Denmark, Djibouti, Dominica, Dominican Republic, Ecuador, Egypt, El Salvador, Equatorial Guinea, Eritrea, Estonia, Ethiopia, Fiji, Finland,

France, Gabon, Gambia, Georgia, Germany, Ghana, Greece, Grenada, Guatemala, Guinea, Guinea-Bissau, Guyana, Haiti, Honduras, Hungary, Iceland, India, Indonesia, Iran, Iraq, Ireland, Italy, Jamaica, Japan, Jordan, Kazakhstan, Kenya, Kiribati, Kuwait, Kyrgyzstan, Lao People's Democratic Republic, Latvia, Lebanon, Lesotho, Liberia, Liechtenstein, Lithuania, Luxembourg, Madagascar, Malawi, Malaysia, Maldives, Mali, Malta, Mauritania, Mauritius, Mexico, Monaco, Mongolia, Montenegro, Morocco, Mozambique, Myanmar, Namibia, Nauru, Nepal, Netherlands, New Zealand, Nicaragua, Niger, Nigeria, Norway, Oman, Pakistan, Panama, Papua New Guinea, Paraguay, Peru, Philippines, Poland, Portugal, Qatar, Republic of Korea, Republic of Moldova, Romania, Russian Federation, Rwanda, Saint Kitts and Nevis, Saint Lucia, Saint Vincent and the Grenadines, Samoa, San Marino, Sao Tome and Principe, Saudi Arabia, Senegal, Serbia, Seychelles, Sierra Leone, Singapore, Slovakia, Slovenia, Solomon Islands, Somalia, South Africa, South Sudan, Spain, Sri Lanka, Sudan, Suriname, Swaziland, Switzerland, Syria, Tajikistan, Thailand, The former Yugoslav Republic of Macedonia, Timor-Leste, Togo, Tonga, Trinidad and Tobago, Tunisia, Turkey, Turkmenistan, Tuvalu, Uganda, Ukraine, United Arab Emirates, United Kingdom, United Republic of Tanzania, Uruguay, Uzbekistan, Vanuatu, Venezuela, Viet Nam, Yemen, Zambia, Zimbabwe.

AGAINST: Israel, United States.

ABSTAIN: Marshall Islands, Micronesia (Federated States of), Palau.

ABSENT: Libya, Sweden.

Bibliography

ABREU, Ramiro J. *En el último año de aquella República*. Havana:
    Editorial de Ciencias Sociales, 1984.

AGUILA, Juan M. del *Cuba : Dilemmas of a Revolution*. Boulder, CO:
    Westview, 1988.

ALZUGARAY, Carlos. *Crónica de un fracaso imperial*. Havana: Editorial
    de Ciencias Sociales, 2000.

AMBROSE, Stephen. *Eisenhower: The President*. New York: Simon &
    Schuster, 1984.

AMIOT, Julie, and Nancy BERTHIER. *Cuba: Cinéma et Révolution*.
    Lyon: GRIMH, 2006.

AYMARIS, Alberto. *Cuba, entorno legal del bloqueo*. Montevideo:
    Fundación de Cultura Universitaria, 1996.

BELL, José, Delia Luisa LOPEZ, and Tania CARAM. *Documentos de
    la Revolución cubana, 1959/* Havana: Editorial de Ciencias
    Sociales, 2006.

BENDER, Lynn Darrell. *The Politics of Hostility: Castro's Revolution and
    United States Policy*. Hato Rey, P.R.: Inter American University
    Press, 1975.

BENJAMIN, Jules Robert. *The United States and the Origins of the
    Cuban Revolution: An Empire for Liberty in an Age of National
    Liberation*. Princeton: Princeton University Press, 1990.

BERNARDINI, Aldo, Flavia LATTANZI, and Marina SPINEDI.
    *Riflessioni sulla conformità o meno al diritto internazionale dell'
    embargo economico commerciale e finanziario attuato dagli Stati
    Uniti nei confronti di Cuba*. Rome: Fondazione Internazionale
    Lelio Basso per il Diritto e la Liberazione dei Popoli, Nova
    Cultura Editrice, Nuova edizione economica, 1992.

BERTHIER, Nancy, and Jean LAMORE. *La Révolution cubaine: Cinéma
    et révolution*. Paris: SEDES-CNED, 2006.

BERTHIER, Nancy. *Fidel Castro: Arrêt sur image*. Paris: Editions
    Ophrys, 2010.

BLASIER, Cole. *The Hovering Giant: U.S. Responses to Revolutionary Change in Latin America*. Pittsburgh: University of Pittsburgh Press, 1976.

BONSAL, Philip W. *Cuba, Castro and the United States*. Pittsburgh: University of Pittsburgh Press, 1971.

BRENNER, Philip. *From Confrontation to Negotiation: U.S. Relations with Cuba*. Boulder, CO: Westview, 1988.

CEPERO BONILLA, Raúl. *Escritos económicos*. Havana: Editorial de Ciencias Sociales, 1983.

CHARADAN LÓPEZ, Fernando. *La industria azucarera en Cuba* Havana: Editorial de Ciencias Sociales, 1982.

COHEN, James, and Françoise MOULIN-CIVIL. *Cuba sous le régime de la Constitution de 1940*. Paris: L'Harmattan, 1997.

COLLAZO PÉREZ, Enrique. *Los americanos en Cuba*. Havana: Editorial de Ciencias Sociales, 1972.

CRASSWELLER, Robert D. *Cuba and the U.S.: The Tangled Relationship*. New York: Foreign Policy Association, 1971.

DILLA, Haroldo, ed. *La democracia en Cuba y el diferendo con los Estados Unidos*. Havana: Ediciones CEA, 1995.

DOMINGUEZ, Jorge I. *Cuba: Order and Revolution*. Cambridge, MA: Harvard University Press, 1978.

_____. *To Make a World Safe for Revolution: Cuba's Foreign Policy*. Cambridge, MA: Harvard University Press, 1989.

DOMINGUEZ, Jorge I., and Rafael HERNÁNDEZ, eds. *U.S.-Cuba Relations in the 1990s*. Boulder, CO: Westview, 1989.

DUMPIERRE, Erasmo. *La ESSO en Cuba: Monopolio y república burguesa*. Havana: Editorial de Ciencias Sociales, 1984.

ECKSTEIN, Susan. *Back from the Future: Cuba under Castro*. Princeton: Princeton University Press, 1994.

EISENHOWER, Dwight D. *The White House Years: Mandate for Change, 1953–1956*. Garden City, NY: Doubleday, 1963.

_____. *The White House Years: Waging Peace, 1956–1961*. Garden City, NY: Doubleday, 1965.

ELLIOT, Jeffrey, and Marvin DYMALLY. *Fidel Castro: Nada podrá detener la marcha de la historia*. Havana; Editora Política, 1985.

ERISMAN, Michael H. *Cuba's International Relations*. Boulder, CO: Westview, 1985.

ESTRADE, Paul. *José Martí: Los fundamentos de la democracia en América Latina*. Madrid: Editorial Doce Calles, 2000.

FONER, Philip Sheldon. *A History of Cuba and Its Relations with the United States*. New York: International Publishers, 1962.

_____. *La Guerra hispano-cubano-americana y el nacimiento del imperialismo norteamericano*. 2 vols. Madrid: Akal Editor, 1975.

FRANKLIN, Jane. *Cuba and the United States: A Chronological History*. Melbourne: Ocean Press, 1997.

FUKUYAMA, Francis. *The End of History and the Last Man*. New York: Avon Books, 1992.

GARCÍA, Alejandro, and Oscar ZANETTI. *United Fruit Company: Un caso del dominio imperialista en Cuba*. Havana: Editorial de Ciencias Sociales, 1976.

GAY-SYLVESTRE, Dominique. *Revolución cubana: Miradas cruzadas (1959–2006)*. Tenerife: Ediciones Idea, Letras de Cuba, 2007.

GLEIJESES, Piero. *Misiones en conflicto. La Habana, Washington y África, 1959–1976*. Havana: Editorial de Ciencias Sociales, 2004.

GOTT, Richard. *Cuba: A New History*. New Haven: Yale University Press, 2004.

GUERRA, Ramiro. *Azúcar y población de las Antillas*. Havana: Editorial de Ciencias Sociales, 1970.

_____. *La Expansión territorial de los Estados Unidos a expensas de España y los demás países latinoamericanos*. Havana: Editorial de Ciencias Sociales, 1975.

GUICHARNOT-TOLLIS, Michèle, ed. *Le Sucre dans l'espace Caraïbe hispanophone*. Paris: L'Harmattan, 1999.

GUICHARNOT-TOLLIS, Michèle, and Jean-Louis JOACHIM. *Cuba, de l'indépendance à nos jours*. Paris: Ellipses, 2007.

HABEL, Janette. *Ruptures à La Havane. Le castrisme en crise*. Paris: La Brèche, 1989.

HERNANDEZ, Sandra, ed. *La Révolution cubaine, mémoires, identités, écritures*. Nantes: Editions du CRINI, 2007.

HERRERA, Rémy. *Cuba révolutionnaire: Histoire et culture*. Paris: L'Harmattan, 2005.

_____. *Cuba révolutionnaire: Economie et planification*. Paris: L'Harmattan, 2006.

HESTON, Thomas J. *Sweet Subsidy: The Economic and Diplomatic Effects of U.S. Sugar Acts, 1934–1974*. New York: Garland, 1987.

HUFBAUER, Gary C., and Jeffrey J. SCHOOT. *Economic Sanctions Reconsidered: History and Current Policy*. 2nd ed. Washington, D.C.: Institute for International Economics, 1990.

JENKS, Leland H. *Our Cuban Colony: A Study in Sugar*. New York: Arno Press and New York Times, 1970.

KAPLOWITZ, Donna Rich. *Anatomy of a Failed Embargo: U.S. Sanctions against Cuba*. Boulder, CO: Lynne Rienner Publishers, 1998.

LAMORE, Jean. *Cuba, que sais-je*. Paris: Presses Universitaires de France, 2007.

_____. *José Martí: La liberté de Cuba et de l'Amérique latine*. Paris: Ellipses, 2007.

_____. *Cuba au cœur de la Révolution: Acteurs et témoins*. Paris: Ellipses, 2006.

_____. *José Martí et l'Amérique*, 2 vols. Paris: L'Harmattan, 1986–1988.

LAMRANI, Salim. *Cuba face à l'Empire*. Outremont: Lanctôt, 2005.

_____. *Washington contre Cuba*. Pantin: Le Temps des Cerises, 2005.

_____. *Fidel Castro, Cuba et les Etats-Unis*. Pantin: Le Temps des Cerises, 2006.

_____. *Double morale: Cuba, l'Union européenne et les droits de l'homme*. Paris: Editions Estrella, 2008.

_____. *Cuba: Ce que les médias ne vous diront jamais*. Paris: Editions Estrella, 2009.

LANGLEY, Lester D. *The Cuban Policy of the United States: A Brief History*. New York: Wiley, 1968.

_____. *The U.S., Cuba, and the Cold War: American Failure or Communist Conspiracy*. Lexington, MA: Heath, 1970.

_____. *The United States and the Caribbean, 1900–1970*. Athens, GA: University of Georgia Press, 1980.

LEMOINE, Maurice. *Cuba: 30 ans de Révolution*. Paris: Autrement, 1989.

LEÓN COTAYO, Nicanor. *El bloqueo a Cuba*. Havana: Editorial de Ciencias Sociales, 1983.

_____. *Sitiada la esperanza*. Havana: Editora Política, 1992.

LE RIVEREND, Julio. *Historia económica de Cuba*. Havana: Editorial Pueblo y Educación, 1981.

LÓPEZ SEGRERA, Francisco. *Cuba: Política exterior y revolución 1959–88*. Havana: I.S.R.I., 1989.

_____. *Cuba, capitalismo dependiente y subdesarrollo (1510–1959)*. Havana: Casa de las Américas, 1976.

MARTÍ, José. *Obras Completas*. Havana: Editorial Nacional de Cuba, 1963.

MINÀ, Gianni. *Un encuentro con Fidel*. Havana: Oficina de Publicaciones del Consejo de Estado, 1987.

MENÉNDEZ, Mario. *Cuba, Haïti et l'interventionnisme américain: Un poids, deux mesures*. Paris: CNRS Editions, Collection Histoire, 2005.

MESA-LAGO, Carmela. *La economía de Cuba socialista*. Madrid: Playor, 1985.

_____. *Breve historia económica de la Cuba socialista*. Madrid: Alianza, 1994.

MIRANDA BRAVO, Olga. *Cuba-U.S.A. Nacionalizaciones y Bloqueo*. Havana: Editorial de Ciencias Sociales, 1996.

MORLEY, Morris H. *Imperial State and Revolution: The United States and Cuba, 1952–1976*. Cambridge: Cambridge University Press, 1997.

MOULIN-CIVIL, Françoise, ed. *Cuba 1956–2006: Révolution dans la culture, Culture dans la révolution*. Paris: L'Harmattan, 2008.

MURRAY, Mary. *Cruel and Unusual Punishment: The U.S. Blockade against Cuba*. New York: Ocean Press, 1992.

NARANJO, Consuelo. *Historia de Cuba*, Aranjuez: Dice Calles, 2009.

ORTIZ, Fernando. *Cuban Counterpoint: Tobacco and Sugar*. New York: Knopf, 1947.

ORTIZ, Jean. *Che plus que jamais*. Biarritz: Éditions Atlantica, 2007.

PATERSON, Thomas G. *Kennedy's Quest for Victory: American Foreign Policy, 1961–1963*. New York: Oxford University Press, 1989.

_____. *Contesting Castro: The United States and the Triumph of the Cuban Revolution*. New York: Oxford University Press, 1994.

PÉREZ, Louis A., Jr. *Cuba and the United States: Ties of Singular Intimacy*. Atlanta: University of Georgia Press, 1997.

PÉREZ LÓPEZ, Jorge F. *The Economics of Sugar*. Pittsburgh: University of Pittsburgh Press, 1991.

PÉREZ STABLE, Marifeli. *The Cuban Revolution: Origins, Course and Legacy*. New York: Oxford University Press, 1994.

PÉREZ VILLANUEVA, Omar E. *La estrategia económica cubana: Medio siglo de socialismo*. Havana: Universidad de La Habana, 2008.

PETRAS, James F., and Robert LAPORTE Jr. *Cultivating Revolution: The United States and Agrarian Reform in Latin America*. New York: Random House, 1971.

PIC-GILLARD, Christine. *Révolutions à Cuba. De José Martí à Fidel Castro*. Paris: Ellipses, 2007.

PINO SANTOS, Oscar. *Los años 1950*. Havana: Editorial Arte y Literatura, 2008.

_____. *Cuba: Historia y economía*. Havana: Editorial de Ciencias Sociales, 1983.

_____. *El asalto a Cuba por la oligarquía financiera yanqui*. Havana: Casa de las Américas, 1973.

_____. *El imperialismo norteamericano en la economía de Cuba*. Havana, Editorial de Ciencias Sociales, 1973.

_____. *Historia de Cuba: Aspectos fundamentales*. Havana: Consejo Nacional de Universidades, 1964.

PONCE, Néstor, ed. *La Révolution cubaine 1959–1992*. Paris: Éditions du Temps, 2006.

RAMONET, Ignacio. *Fidel Castro, biographie à deux voix*. Paris: Fayard/Galilée, 2006.

ROIG DE LEUCHSENRING, Emilio. *Cuba no debe su independencia a los Estados Unidos*. Havana: Editorial de Ciencias Sociales, 1950.

SMITH, Wayne S. *The Closest of Enemies: A Personal and Diplomatic Account of U.S.-Cuban Relations since 1957*. New York and London: W. W. Norton, 1987.

SMITH, Wayne S., and Esteban MORALES DOMINGUEZ, eds. *Subject to Solution: Problems in Cuba-U.S. Relations*. Boulder, CO: Lynne Rienner Publishers, 1988.

TAIBO II, Paco Ignacio. *Ernesto Guevara connu aussi comme le Che*. Paris: Métailié/Payot, 1997.

THOMAS, Hugh. *Cuba, the Pursuit of Freedom*. New York: Harper and Row, 1971.

_____. *The Cuban Revolution*. New York: Harper and Row, 1977.

VALDÉS, Nelson P., and Edwin LIEUWEN. *The Cuban Revolution*. Albuquerque: University of New Mexico Press, 1971.

WELCH, Richard E., Jr. *Response to Revolution: The United States and the Cuban Revolution, 1959–1961*. Chapel Hill: University of North Carolina Press, 1985.

ZINN, Howard. *A People's History of the United States*. 1980; repr. New York: HarperCollins, 1995.

ZUAZNABAR, Ismael. *La economía cubana en la década del 50*. Havana: Editorial de Ciencias Sociales, 1986.

Notes

EDITOR'S NOTE: Cuban websites may not be accessible from the United States. To access French websites, you have to set your browser to French.

1. U.S. Government Accountability Office, *Economic Sanctions: Agencies Face Competing Priorities in Enforcing the U.S. Embargo on Cuba*, November 2007, www.gao.gov/new.items/d0880.pdf.

2. Ibid.

3. S. Everett Gleason, "Memorandum of Discussion at the 392nd Meeting of the National Security Council, Washington," December 23, 1958, *Foreign Relations of the United States*, 1991, Eisenhower Library, Whitman File, NSC Records, Top Secret, Eyes Only, 302–3.

4. José Bell, Delia Luisa López, and Tania Caram, *Documentos de la Revolución cubana, 1959* (Havana: Editorial de Ciencias Sociales, 2006), 16–18.

5. Central Intelligence Agency, "NSC Briefing: Cuba," January 6, 1959, Freedom of Information Act case no. CSI-1998-00005, release date February 6, 1998.

6. Salim Lamrani, *Fidel Castro, Cuba et les États-Unis* (Pantin, Fr.: Le Temps des Cerises, 2006), 123.

7. Paco Ignacio Taibo II, *Ernesto Guevara connu aussi comme le Che* (Paris: Métailié/Payot, 1997), 369.

8. Constitution of 1940, Republic of Cuba, *Political Database of the Americas*, University of Georgetown, http://pdba.georgetown.edu/constitutions/cuba/cuba1940.html.

9. Ricardo Alarcón de Quesada, "Discurso del co. Ricardo Alarcón de Quesada en las Naciones Unidas," Cuban Parliament, November 9, 1999, www.parlamentocubano.cu/index.php?option=com_content&view=article&id=425:discurso-del-co-ricardo-alarcon-de-quesada-en-las-naciones-unidas-el-91199-tema-sobre-el-bloqueo&catid=65:discursos-e-intervenciones-presidente-anpp&Itemid=112.

10. Lamrani, *Fidel Castro, Cuba et les États-Unis*, 122.

11. Fidel Castro Ruz, "Discurso pronunciado por el Comandante Fidel Castro Ruz, Primer Ministro del Gobierno Revolucionario, en la

sede de las Naciones Unidas," September 26, 1960, http://www.cuba.cu/gobierno/discursos/1960/esp/f260960e.html (website consulted on June 2, 2011).

12. Nuria Pérez and Vilma Ponce Suárez, *Incidencias del bloqueo del gobierno de los Estados Unidos en las bibliotecas cubanas: 2001–2005,* José Martí Library, 2006, http://www.abinia.org/informe-cuba.pdf, 55.

13. Hugh, Thomas, *Cuba: The Pursuit of Freedom* (New York: Harper & Row, 1971), 224, 252.

14. Frank G. Dawson and Burns H. Weston, "'Prompt, Adequate and Effective': A Universal Standard of Compensation?," 30 *Fordham Law Review* 30/4 (1962): 727; http://ir.lawnet.fordham.edu/flr/vol30/iss4/4.

15. United Nations Charter, Article 2(1), June 26, 1945; www.afnu.org/fileadmin/templates/www.afnu.org/pdf/doc_charte_onu.pdf.

16. United Nations General Assembly, "Droit d'exploiter librement les richesses et ressources naturelles," Resolution 626, December 21, 1952. http://www.un.org/french/documents/view_doc.asp?symbol=A/RES/626percent28VIIpercent29&Lang=F.

17. Ibid.

18. International Court of Justice, *Statut de la Cour Internationale de Justice,* Article 38. http://www.icj-cij.org/documents/index.php?p1=4&p2=2&p3=0&lang=fr.

19. United Nations General Assembly, "Resolution 1803: Souveraineté permanente sur les ressources naturelles," December 14, 1962; http://www.aidh.org/Biblio/Trait_internat/Auto_2.htm.

20. Ibid.

21. United Nations General Assembly, "Charte des droits et devoirs économiques des Etats," Resolution 3281, December 12, 1974.; http://www.un.org/french/documents/view_doc.asp?symbol=A/RES/3281percent28XXIXpercent29&Lang=F.

22. *Cuba vs. Bloqueo,* "Los convenios de pago de reclamaciones celebrados por Cuba (1967–1986)," http://www.cubavsbloqueo.cu/Default.aspx?tabid=69.

23. Brig. General Andrew Goodpaster, "Memorandum of a Conference with the President, White House, Washington," March 17, 1960, *Foreign Relations of the United States,* 1958–1960, Eisenhower Library, Project "Clean Up" Records, Intelligence Matters, Top Secret, 861–63.

24. Cuba vs Bloqueo, " Cronología : Dwight D. Eisenhower (R) (1953–1959–1961)," www.cubavsbloqueo.cu/Default.aspx?tabid=53.

25. Ibid.

26. Jesús M. García Molina, *La economía cubana desde el siglo XVI al XX: Del colonialismo al socialismo con mercado* (Mexico: Comisión Económica Para América Latina y el Caribe, February 2005), 23.

27. *Cuba vs. Bloqueo*, "El proceso de nacionalizaciones en Cuba," http://www.cubavsbloqueo.cu/Default.aspx?tabid=68.

28. Pérez and Suárez, *Incidencias del bloqueo del gobierno de los Estados Unidos en las bibliotecas cubanas*, 56.

29. Congressional Research Service, *Foreign Assistance Act of 1961*, http://www.nationalaglawcenter.org/assets/crs/R40089.pdf.

30. U.S. Code, "Trading with the Enemy Act of 1917," http://www.law.cornell.edu/uscode/html/uscode50a/usc_sup_05_50_10_sq1.html. Since the reform of 1977, which stipulates that the law only applies in time of war, this measure was extended each year by all U.S. presidents from Jimmy Carter to Barack Obama. Cuba is the only country subjected to sanctions under the Trading with the Enemy Act.

31. John F. Kennedy, " Proclamation 3447: Embargo on All Trade with Cuba," *American Presidency Project*, February 3, 1962; http://www.presidency.ucsb.edu/ws/?pid=58824#axzz1PMB9WbnC; "Good Medicine for Cuba," *New York Times*, March 8, 1978.

32. International Committee of the Red Cross, "Convention (IV) relative to the protection of civilian persons in time of war, Geneva, August 12, 1949," http://www.icrc.org/ihl.nsf/full/380.

33. "Leak in Embargo Closed; U.S. Will Bar Goods Shipped through Third Countries," *New York Times*, March 24, 1962.

34. Morris Morley, *Imperial State and Revolution. The United States and Cuba, 1952–1986* (Cambridge: Cambridge University Press, 1988), 202.

35. Louis A. Pérez Jr., *Cuba: Between Reform and Revolution* (New York: Oxford University Press, 1995), 346.

36. *Cuba Debate*, "Cuba eliminará gradualmente libreta de abastecimiento," December 17, 2010.

37. U.S. Department of the Treasury, Office of Foreign Assets Control, "What You Need To Know about the US embargo: An Overview of the Cuban Assets," www.treasury.gov/resource-center/sanctions/Documents/penalty.pdf; and "Cuba Sanctions," www.treasury.gov/resource-center/sanctions/Programs/Pages/cuba.aspx.

38. *Cuba vs. Bloqueo*, "Cronología: Lyndon B. Johnson," http://www. cubavsbloqueo.cu/Default.aspx?tabid=55.

39. Tad Szulc, "Cuba and Guantánamo; Many Diplomats Feel Castro Set Trap and Johnson Administration Fell into It," *New York Times*, February 13, 1964.

40. In 1960, Cuba sold sugar to a U.S. company that subsequently refused to pay because the sugar in question came from a nationalized property. The case came before the courts. *Banco Nacional de Cuba vs. Sabbatino*, 376 US 398 (1964), http://supreme.justia.com/ us/376/398/case.html.

41. Ibid.

42. U.S. Code, "Hickenlooper Amendment," Title 22, Chapter 32, Sub-chapter III, Part I, Sec. 2370, www.law.cornell.edu/uscode/22/2370.

43. Organization of American States, Charter, June 10, 1993, Articles 19 and 20. http://www.cidh.oas.org/Basicos/French/q. Chartepercent20OEA.htm.

44. Thomas J. Hamilton, "Castro Denounces O.A.S. Vote over Sanctions; Castro Assails Action by O.A.S," *New York Times*, July 27, 1964.

45. Morley, *Imperial State and Revolution*, 719.

46. Felix Belair, Jr., "Administration Is Fighting Curb on Food Aid to Other Countries," *New York Times*, May 23 , 1966.

47. *Cuba vs. Bloqueo*, "Cronología: Lyndon B. Johnson."

48. *Cuba vs. Bloqueo*, "Cronología: Richard M. Nixon," http://www. cubavsbloqueo.cu/Default.aspx?tabid=56.

49. *Cuba vs. Bloqueo*, "Cronología: Gerald R. Ford," http://www. cubavsbloqueo.cu/Default.aspx?tabid=57.

50. "Carter Will Not Block Move to Ease Cuba Trade," *New York Times*, April 20, 1977; "McGovern, Back from Cuba, Says He Will Seek the End of Trade Ban," *New York Times*, April 12, 1977.

51. "Senate Panel Votes to Allow Cuba to Buy U.S. Food and Medicine," *New York Times*, May 11, 1977.

52. *Cuba vs. Bloqueo*, "Cronología: James Carter," http://www. cubavsbloqueo.cu/Default.aspx?tabid=58.

53. Graham Hovey, "U.S. and Cuba Ready to Announce Limited Exchange of Diplomats; U.S. and Havana Plan Diplomatic Missions," *New York Times*, June 3, 1977.

54. Wayne S. Smith, *The Closest of Enemies: A Personal and Diplomatic Account of US-Cuban Relations since 1957* (New York: W. W. Norton, 1987).

55. Dena Kleiman, "An Eastern Jet Is Hijacked to Cuba on Flight from Kennedy to Miami," *New York Times*, August 27, 1980; "33 on Jet Returned to Florida after Hijacking to Cuba; Inquiry on Airport Security Treaty on Passenger Return," *New York Times*, August 11, 1980.

56. *Cuba vs. Bloqueo*, "Cronología: Ronald Reagan," http://www.cubavsbloqueo.cu/Default.aspx?tabid=59.

57. U.S Congress, "Omnibus Trade and Competitiveness Act of 1988," August 23, 1988, http://gsi.nist.gov/global/docs/Omnibus.pdf.

58. Smith, *The Closest of Enemies*, 238–66.

59. U.S. Congress, "Omnibus Trade and Competitiveness Act of 1988."

60. U.S. Department of State, "Cuban Democracy Act of 1992," http://www.state.gov/www/regions/wha/cuba/democ_act_1992.html.

61. Economic Commission for Latin America and the Caribbean (ECLAC), *The Cuban Economy: Structural Reforms and Economic Performance in the 1990s* (Mexico: United Nations, December 6, 2001), 22.

62. H. Scott Fairley, "Between Scylla and Charybdis: The U.S. Embargo of Cuba and Canadian Foreign Extraterritorial Measures against It," American Bar Association, October 28, 2009, http://apps.americanbar.org/intlaw/fall09/materials/Fairley_Scott_Damed%20if%20You%20Do.pdf.

63. Lamrani, *Fidel Castro, Cuba et les États-Unis*, 140.

64. Wayne S. Smith, "Cuba's Long Reform," *Foreign Affairs* (March–April 1996).

65. U.S. Department of State, Cuban Democracy Act of 1992.

66. Ibid.

67. *New York Times*, July 15, 1992.

68. Jerry Gray, "President Agrees to Tough New Set of Curbs on Cuba," *New York Times*, February 29, 1996.

69. Jean-Guy Allard, "Basulto confiesa haber disparado cañonazos contra un hotel de La Habana," *Granma*, December 13, 2005, http://www.granma.cu/espanol/2005/diciembre/mar13/51basulto-e.html.

70. Gray, "President Agrees to Tough New Set of Curbs on Cuba."

71. Library of Congress, "Cuban Liberty and Democratic Solidarity (LIBERTAD) Act of 1996," http://thomas.loc.gov/cgi-bin/query/z?c104:H.R.927.ENR.

72. Ibid.

73. Aynel Alvarez Guerra and Anet Pino Rivero, "Análisis jurídico sobre la ilegalidad del bloqueo impuesto a Cuba por los Estados Unidos,"

Dirección Jurídica del Ministerio de Relaciones Exteriores de la República de Cuba, *Cuba vs. Bloqueo*, http://www.cubavsbloqueo. cu/Default.aspx?tabid=63.

74. Library of Congress, "Cuban Liberty and Democratic Solidarity."

75. Ibid.

76. Ibid.

77. Ibid.

78. Guerra and Rivero, "Análisis jurídico sobre la ilegalidad del bloqueo impuesto a Cuba por los Estados Unidos."

79. *Cuba vs. Bloqueo*, "Cronología: William Clinton."

80. Paolo Spadoni, "The Impact of the Helms-Burton Legislation on Foreign Investment in Cuba," Association for the Study of the Cuban Economy, August 2–4, 2001, 29, http://www.ascecuba. org/publications/proceedings/volume11/pdfs/spadoni.pdf.

81. Daniel W. Fisk, "Anticipando el día en que Cuba será libre," Departamento de Estado de los Estados Unidos, October 9, 2004, http://dosfan.lib.uic.edu/spanish/col/d/38198.htm.

82. David Stout, "U.S. Says Cuba Causes Misery with Its Hard Line," *New York Times*, August 29, 2000.

83. U.S. Department of Agriculture, "Trade Sanctions Reform and Export Enhancement Act of 2000," www.fas.usda.gov/itp/cuba/ title_ix.html; Center for International Policy, "U.S. Agricultural Trade with Cuba," http://ciponline.org/cuba/trade/tradeembargo. htm. In March 2009, the Obama administration eased these restrictions and permitted Cuba to pay for imports after delivery.

84. John R. Coleman, *U.S. Agricultural Sales to Cuba: Certain Economic Effects of U.S. Restrictions*, U.S. International Trade Commission, June 2009, 2; http://www.usitc.gov/publications/332/working_ papers/ID-22.pdf.

85. *Cuba vs. Bloqueo*, "Cronología: George W. Bush."

86. U.S. International Trade Commission, *U.S. Agricultural Sales to Cuba: Certain Economic Effects of U.S. Restrictions*, July 2007, 49; http://www.usitc.gov/publications/332/pub3932.pdf.

87. Cuba Policy Foundation, "America's Farmers Bearing Heavy Burden for U.S. Embargo against Cuba: New Report," February 28, 2002; http://www.cubafoundation.org/pdf/CPF-Release-Ag Study-0202.28.

88. Sen. Ben Nelson, "Nelson Urges President to Lift Agricultural Trade Restrictions with Cuba," September 28, 2010, http://bennelson. senate.gov/press/press_releases/092810-02.cfm..

89. U.S. Department of the Treasury, "Treasury Designates and Blocks Entities for Cuban Embargo Violations," February 2, 2004, http://www.treasury.gov/press-center/press-releases/Pages/js1161.aspx.

90. Alicia Rivera, "EE UU prohíbe publicar artículos científicos de Cuba, Irán, Libia y Sudán," El País, February 24, 2004.

91. Douglas Starr, "Tightening the Screws on Cuba," Boston Globe, May 18, 2004; BBC News, "US blocks Cuban Grammy Nominees," February 6, 2004.

92. U.S. Citizenship and Immigration Services, "Immigration and Nationality Act," March 4, 2010.

93. Cuba vs. Bloqueo, "Cronología: Barack Obama," http://www.cubavsbloqueo.cu/Default.aspx?tabid=3381.

94. Colin L. Powell, Commission for Assistance to a Free Cuba (Washington, D.C.: U.S. Department of State, May 2004).

95. Ibid., 41.

96. Human Rights Watch, "Families Torn Apart, " February 3, 2009, http://www.hrw.org/en/node/80478/section/2.

97. Powell, Commission for Assistance to a Free Cuba, 22.

98. Editors, "Election-Year Cuba Policy," New York Times, June 27, 2004.

99. "Leader: A Cuban Dead-End," Financial Times, May 10, 2004.

100. Condoleezza Rice and Carlos Gutierrez, Commission for Assistance to a Free Cuba (Washington, D.C.: U.S. Department of State, July, 2006), http://www.cafc.gov/documents/organization/68166.pdf.

101. Ibid.

102. Ibid.

103. Ibid.

104. Ricardo Alarcón de Quesada, "El Plan de Bush de 'asistencia a una Cuba libre': Crónica de una guerra anunciada, " Granma, July 5, 2006.

105. Wilfredo Cancio Isla, "Crean grupo para reforzar embargo a Cuba," El Nuevo Herald, October 11, 2006; "U.S. to Step Up Cuba Sanction Enforcement," South Florida Business Journal, October 10, 2006; Jay Weaver, "New Task Force to Target Cuba Bans Offenders," Miami Herald, October 11, 2006.

106. Ibid.

107. Ibid.

108. Associated Press, "Obama Seeks 'New Beginning' with Cuba," April 17, 2009.

109. Barack Obama, "Our Main Goal : Freedom in Cuba," Miami Herald, August 21, 2007.

110. U.S. Treasury Department, Office of Foreign Assets Control, "Hoja informativa: Tesoro modifica reglamento para el control de bienes cubanos a fin de implementar el programa del Presidente sobre visitas familiares, remesas y telecomunicaciones," September 3, 2009.

111. John Dorschner and Monica Hatcher, "Liberan a los viajes a Cuba," *El Nuevo Herald,* April 13, 2009.

112. Ginger Thomson, "U.S. Official Meets with Cuban Authorities," *New York Times,* September 30, 2009.

113. Office of Ricardo Alarcón de Quesada, September 22, 2009; Agence France Presse, "Cuba asegura que EEUU impidió viaje de 30 científicos," September 23, 2009; Agencia Cubana de Noticias, "Washington Bans Orthopedic Doctors from Attending Event in Cuba," September 22, 2009; Jim Abrams, "Senador intercede por permiso de viaje para la Filarmónica de NY," Associated Press, October 5, 2009.

114. U.S. Department of Commerce, Bureau of Industry and Security, "2011 Report on Foreign Policy-Based Export Controls," http://www.bis.doc.gov/news/2011/2011_fpreport.pdf, 37.

115. Bruno Rodríguez Parilla, Minister of Foreign Affairs, Cuba, "Discurso de Bruno Rodríguez Parrilla, Ministro de Relaciones Exteriores de la República de Cuba en la sesión de la Asamblea General de las Naciones Unidas, en el Tema 'Necesidad de poner fin al Bloqueo económico, comercial y financiero impuesto por los Estados Unidos de América contra Cuba,'" UN General Assembly, October 26, 2010.

116. *Cuba vs. bloqueo,* "Informe de Cuba sobre la resolución 64/6 de la Asamblea General de las Naciones Unidas," 2010, http://www.cubavsbloqueo.cu/Informe2010/2.html.

117. Parilla, "Discurso de Bruno Rodríguez Parrilla."

118. *Cuba vs. bloqueo,* "Informe de Cuba sobre la resolución 64/6."

119. Ibid.

120. Ibid.

121. José de la Osa, "Impide Estados Unidos a Cuba compra de anestésicos para niños," *Granma,* May 3, 2011.

122. Ministry of Foreign Affairs, Cuba, "Informe de Cuba sobre la resolución 64/6," *Cuba vs. bloqueo,* http://www.cubavsbloqueo.cu/Informe2010/2.html.

123. U.S. Department of the Treasury, "OFAC Civil Penalties Enforcement Information," June 4, 2004, www.treasury.gov/resource-center/sanctions/OFAC-Enforcement/Documents/06042004.pdf.

124. U.S. District Court for the Eastern District of Pennsylvania, *United States of America, Appellant, v. Stefan E. Brodie*, April 12, 2005; http://174.123.24.242/leagle/xmlResult.aspx?xmldoc=20055264 03F3d123_1513.xml&docbase=CSLWAR2-1986-2006.

125. "Denuncia Cuba incautación de fondos por EE.UU. en sector de la salud," *Prensa Latina*, March 11, 2011.

126. Emilie Lembrée, "Cuba," *Amnesty International*, May 13, 2011; http://www.amnestyinternational.be/doc/s-informer/les-rapports-annuels/le-rapport-annuel-2011/ameriques-2092/article/cuba-17804.

127. Inter-American Commission on Human Rights, *2010 Annual Report, Status of Human Rights in Cuba*, 4:436; http://www.cidh.oas.org/annualrep/2010eng/TOC.htm.

128. Amnesty International, *The US Embargo against Cuba: Its Impact on Economic and Social Rights*, 2009, http://www.amnesty.org/en/library/asset/AMR25/007/2009/en/51469f8b-73f8-47a2-a5bd-f839adf50488/amr250072009eng.pdf, 5, 6.

129. Human Rights Council, "Situation of Human Rights in Cuba," report submitted by the Personal Representative of the High Commissioner for Human Rights, Christine Chanet, January 26, 2007.   http://www2.ohchr.org/english/countries/cu/mandate/index.htm, A/HRC/4/12, para. 7.

130. American Association for World Health, "Denial of Food and Medicine: The Impact of the U.S. Embargo on Health and Nutrition in Cuba," Interreligious Foundation for Community Organization, March 1997.

131. Leon Eisenberg, "The Sleep of Reason Produces Monsters— Human Cost of Economic Sanctions," *New England Journal of Medicine*, April 24, 1997, 1248–50.

132. Fitzhugh Mullan, "Affirmative Action, Cuba Style," *New England Journal of Medicine* (December 23, 2004): 2682.

133. Center for Constitutional Rights, "American Couple Sue US Treasury Department for Unreasonable Penalties in Cuba Travel Case," April 23, 2003, http://www.commondreams.org/news2003/0422-05.htm.

134. Douglas Starr, "Tightening the Screws on Cuba," *Boston Globe*, May 18, 2004.

135. Anne Wallace Allen, "Retirees Fined for Traveling to Cuba to Research Book," Associated Press, April 20, 2004.

136. Easterbrook, Evans, and Williams, circuit judges, *United States of America v. Richard S. Connors*, March 21, 2006, http://openjurist. org/441/f3d/527/united-states-v-s-connors.
137. Gerardo Reyes, "Mano dura con los violadores del embargo a Cuba," *El Nuevo Herald*, June 11, 2004.
138. Jennifer Babson, "Keys Boaters Cleared of Embargo Charges," *Miami Herald*, October 30, 2004.
139. Frank Martin, "Bush castiga a religiosos por venir a Cuba," *Granma*, June 17, 2004.
140. "Doctor Faces Fine for Buying Cuban Dolphins," *Los Angeles Times*, August 30, 2004.
141. Charles D. Sherman, "Doctor Fined $70,000 for Buying Cuban Dolphins," *Miami Herald*, August 28, 2004.
142. Biblioteca José Martí, "Cronología de las medidas y pronunciamientos relacionados con el bloqueo contra Cuba y sus bibliotecas en el periodo 2001–2005," 150; http://www.bnjm.cu/ sitios/laverdaddecuba/bloqueo/pdf/VII_parte.pdf.
143. Reuters, "Benjamin Treuhaft—OFAC-Defying Piano Tuner," May 18, 2006.
144. Max Baucus, "Baucus Calls Bush Cuba Policy 'Absurd,'" *U.S. Senate*, May 6, 2004; www.senate.gov/~baucus/Press/04/05/2004506 C41.html.
145. Olga Miranda Bravo, "¿Por qué Bloqueo y no embargo," *Cuba vs. bloqueo*, http://www.cubavsbloqueo.cu/Default.aspx?tabid=65. See also Olga Miranda Bravo, *Cuba-USA: Nacionalizaciones y Bloqueo* (Havana: Editorial de Ciencias Sociales, 1996).
146. Andrea Rodriguez, "Cuba satisfecha porque Iberoamérica habla de 'bloqueo,'" *El Nuevo Herald*, October 17, 2005.
147. ICRC, Declaration Concerning the Laws of Naval War, London, February 26, 1909, http://www.icrc.org/ihl.nsf/ FULL/255?OpenDocument.
148. Ministry of Foreign Affairs, France, "Blocus," http://www. diplomatie.gouv.fr/fr/ministere_817/archives-patrimoine_3512/ fonds-collections_5143/archives-affaires-etrangeres_11591/admin- istration-centrale_11601/affaires-economiques-commerciales_ 11612/blocus_13329/blocus_29435.html.
149. Bravo, "¿Por qué Bloqueo y no embargo."
150. UN General Assembly, "Déclaration relative au principe du droit international touchant les relations amicales et la coopération entre les Etats conformément à la charte des Nations unies," October

24, 1970, in "Résolutions adoptées sur les rapports de la sixième commission," UN, 25th session, 1970; http://www.un.org/french/documents/view_doc.asp?symbol=A/RES/2625percent28XXVpercent29&Lang=F.

151. Felipe Pérez Roque, Minister of Foreign Affairs, Cuba, "Declaración del Excelentísimo Señor Felipe Pérez Roque, Ministro de Relaciones Exteriores de la República de Cuba, en el tema 28 de la agenda de la Asamblea General de la ONU : Necesidad de poner fin al bloqueo económico, comercial y financiero impuesto por los Estados Unidos de America contra Cuba," October 28, 2004; http://embacuba.cubaminrex.cu/Default.aspx?tabid=3045.

152. Reuters, "ING Unit Put on US Blacklist for Cuba Business," October 3, 2006.

153. U.S. Department of the Treasury, "OFAC Civil Penalties Enforcement Information," December 3, 2004; http://www.treasury.gov/resource-center/sanctions/OFAC-Enforcement/Documents/12032004.pdf.

154. Marc P. Sullivan, U.S. Department of State, "Cuba: Issues for the 109th Congress," January 23, 2006,16; http://fpc.state.gov/documents/organization/61636.pdf.

155. Inigo Moré, "US Imposes Fine on Iberia for Breaking Cuba Embargo," *Financial Times*, September 2, 2004. After negotiations, the fine was reduced to $8,000.

156. Felipe Pérez Roque, "La memoria corta dell'occidente," *Latinoamerica* 93 (November 8, 2005): 54.

157. Ibid.

158. U.S. Department of the Treasury, "Cuban Cigar Update," September 30, 2004, http://www.treasury.gov/resource-center/sanctions/Documents/ccigar2.pdf.

159. Pablo Bachelet, "U.S.-Owned Hotel Could Face Fines," *Miami Herald*, February 8, 2006.

160. "Cuba Says Scotiabank Has Broken Int'l Law," *Jamaica Gleaner*, April 5, 2006.

161. Ana Aoki, "Interview de Jorge Jorge González," *Jiji Press*, October 2006.

162. "Hotel noruego comprado por la Hilton niega hospedaje a misión cubana," January 5, 2007.

163. Ibid.

164. EFE, "El embargo a Cuba salpica a Austria: La cancelación de cuentas de cubanos en un banco adquirido por un fondo de EE UU abre un encendido debate," April 18, 2007.

165. World Data Service, "Anuncia gobierno de Austria medidas contra banco que se unió a bloqueo anticubano," April 20, 2007.

166. Reuters, "BAWAG Restores Cuban Accounts after Public Uproar," May 4, 2007; Associated Press, "Banco austríaca reanuda transacciones con ciudadanos cubanos," May 4, 2007.

167. Gabriel Molina, "Austria apuesta por la soberanía," *Granma*, May 7, 2007.

168. "EEUU fuerza a la compañía Hola Airlines a abandonar Cuba," *Diario de Mallorca*, July 12, 2007.

169. Adam Liptak, "A Wave of the Watch List, and Speech Disappears," *New York Times*, March 4, 2008.

170. U.S. Department of the Treasury, OFAC, "Settlement Agreement between the U.S. Department of the Treasury's Office of Foreign Assets Control and Australia and New Zealand Banking Group, Ltd., and Its Subsidiaries," August 24, 2009; http://www.treasury.gov/resource-center/sanctions/OFAC-Enforcement/Documents/anz_08242009.pdf.

171. OFAC, "Settlement Agreement between the U.S. Department of the Treasury's Office of Foreign Assets Control and Credit Suisse AG," December 16, 2009; http://www.treasury.gov/resource-center/sanctions/OFAC-Enforcement/Documents/12162009.pdf.

172. OFAC, "Settlement Agreement between the U.S. Department of the Treasury's Office of Foreign Assets Control and Iimospec, Inc., a Delaware Corporation," March 10, 2010; http://www.treasury.gov/resource-center/sanctions/OFAC-Enforcement/Documents/innospec_ag.pdf.

173. Ministry of Foreign Affairs, Cuba, "Informe de Cuba sobre la resolución 64/6," *Cuba vs bloqueo*, 1.3; http://www.cubavsbloqueo.cu/Informe2010/1_3.html.

174. OFAC, "Settlement Agreement ING," June 2012. http://www.treasury.gov/resource-center/sanctions/CivPen/Documents/06122012_ing_agreement.pdf.

175. Ministry of Foreign Affairs, Cuba, "Statement by the Ministry of Foreign Affairs," June 20, 2012; http://www.cubaminrex.cu/english/Statements/Articulos/StatementsMINREX/2012/Statement200612.html.

176. Ibid.

177. Steve Stecklow and Bail Katz, "U.S. to Fine Ericsson in Panama $1.75 Million over Cuba Shipments," Reuters, May 24, 2012.

178. OFAC, "Enforcement Information for July 10, 2012," July 10, 2012; http://www.treasury.gov/resource-center/sanctions/CivPen/Documents/07102012_great_western.pdf.

179. Jean da Luz, "Carlson Wagonlit Travel: l'embargo cubain fait tomber des têtes en France," *Tourmag*, July 2, 2012; Geneviève Bieganowsky, "Licienciements, Carlson redoute la perte des budgets voyages de l'administration US," *Tourmag*, July 3, 2012.

180. Ibid.

181. U.S. Government Accountability Office, "About GAO," http://www.gao.gov/about/index.html.

182. U.S. Government Accountability Office, *Economic Sanctions. Agencies Face Competing Priorities in Enforcing the U.S. Embargo on Cuba*, Report to Congressional Requesters, November 2007, http://www.gao.gov/new.items/d0880.pdf, Introduction, 1, 6.

183. Ibid.

184. Ibid., 6.

185. Ibid., 18.

186. Ibid., 44.

187. Ibid.

188. Ibid., 6.

189. Ibid., 45–46.

190. Ibid., 7.

191. Ibid., 9.

192. Ibid., 48.

193. Ibid., 7–8.

194. James Carter, "Trip Report by Former U.S. President Jimmy Carter, March 28–30, 2011," Carter Center, Atlanta, GA, April 1, 2011, http://www.cartercenter.org/news/trip_reports/cuba-march2011.html.

195. Christopher Hitchens, "What Was Bill Thinking?," *Newsweek*, September 24, 2009, http://www.newsweek.com/id/216052/.

196. Sen. Richard Lugar, http://lugar.senate.gov/sfrc/pdf/Cuba.pdf; Anne Flaherty, "EEUU debe replantear su embargo a Cuba dice senador republicano," Associated Press, February 23, 2009; Wilfredo Cancio Isla, "Informe del Senado pide levantar prohibición de viajes a Cuba antes de abril," *El Nuevo Herald*, February 23, 2009.

197. Wilfredo Cancio Isla, "Congresistas demócratas viajan a Cuba a abrir diálogo," *El Nuevo Herald*, April 2, 2009.

198. AFL-CIO, "Supporting the Repeal of U.S. Travel Restrictions to Cuba and of the U.S. Economic Embargo," September 2009, http://

www.aflcio.org/aboutus/thisistheaflcio/convention/2009/
upload/res_43.pdf.

199. U.S. Chamber of Commerce, "Testimony on 'Examining the Status
of U.S. Trade with Cuba and Its Impact on Economic Growth',"
April 27, 2009, http://www.uschamber.com/sites/default/files/
testimony/090427tradecuba.pdf.

200. Nestor Ikeda, "Dueños de empresas y congresistas piden comercio
con Cuba," Associated Press, May 6, 2009.

201. "Obama, Cuba and the OAS," New York Times, June 4, 2009.

202. "The Useless Cuban Embargo," Los Angeles Times, October 29,
2008.

203. Michael Kinsley, "The Cuba Embargo a Proven Failure," Washington
Post, April 17, 2009.

204. Tim Bearden, "Helms-Burton Act: Resurrecting the Iron Curtain,"
Center on Hemispheric Affairs, June 10, 2011; http://www.coha.
org/helms-burton-act-resurrecting-the-iron-curtain/; Ian Vasquez,
"The Cuba Embargo at 50," Cato Institute, October 18, 2010;
http://www.cato-at-liberty.org/the-cuba-embargo-at-50/.

205. Daniel Griswold, "The US Embargo of Cuba Is a Failure," Guardian,
June 15, 2009.

206. Anya Landau French, Options for Engagement: A Resource Guide
for Reforming U.S. Policy toward Cuba, Lexington Institute, April
2009, www.cubasource.org/pdf/lexingtoninstitute_engagement_
usacuba.pdf, 49.

207. Fidel Castro Ruz, "Militares con criterios acertados," Cuba Debate,
April 15, 2009.

208. Ministry of Foreign Affairs, Cuba, "Informe de Cuba sobre la
resolución 64/6," Cuba vs. bloqueo, 5.1; http://www.cubavsbloqueo.
cu/Informe2010/5.html.

209. "Cuba califica de genocida bloqueo impuesto por Estados Unidos,"
Prensa Latina, September 27, 2005.

210. UN, Office of the High Commissioner on Human Rights,
Convention pour la prévention et la répression du crime de
génocide, December 9, 1948, http://www2.ohchr.org/french/
law/genocide.htm.

211. Lester D. Mallory, "Memorandum from the Deputy Assistant
Secretary of State for Inter-American Affairs (Mallory) to the
Assistant Secretary of State for Inter-American Affairs (Rubottom),"
April 6, 1960, U.S. Department of State, Central Files, 737.00/4-
660, Secret, drafted by Mallory, in Foreign Relations of the United

States (FRUS), 1958–1960, vol. 6, Cuba (Washington, D.C.: U.S. Government Printing Office, 1991), 885.

212. Roque, "Declaración," October 28, 2004.

213. Parilla, "Discurso de Bruno Rodríguez Parrilla," October 26, 2010.

214. UN General Assembly, "187 Etats membres votent pour la levée de l'embargo imposé par les Etats-Unis à Cuba depuis 1962," October 26, 2010, http://www.un.org/News/fr-press/docs/2010/AG11015.doc.htm.

215. Roque, "Declaración," October 28, 2004.

216. Piero Gleijeses, *Misiones en conflicto: La Habana, Washington y África, 1959–1976* (Havana: Editorial de Ciencias Sociales, 2004).

217. José Martí, "Carta a Manuel Mercado," *Portal José Martí*, May 18, 1895; http://www.josemarti.cu/?q=obras&catobra=Cartas&catsubobra=Manuelpercent20Mercado&nid=1637.

218. Francis Fukuyama, *The End of History and the Last Man* (New York: Avon Books, 1992).

219. José Martí, *Obras Completas* (Havana: Editorial Nacional de Cuba, 1963).

220. "Resultados de las votaciones en la ONU en contra del genocida bloqueo económico de Estados Unidos contra Cuba," *Cuba vs. bloqueo*, 2010; http://www.cubavsbloqueo.cu/Default.aspx?tabid=1596.

221. UN, "General Assembly, for Twentieth Year, Demands Lifting of Economic Blockade," October 25, 2011; http://www.un.org/News/Press/docs/2011/ga11162.doc.htm.

Index